Wo  Empo..........

and Entrepreneurial Revolution

The Solution for a Prosperous Society, Poverty Eradication and Wealth Creation

Peter Osalor

Women Empowerment and Entrepreneurial Revolution:
The Solution for a Prosperous Society, Poverty Eradication and Wealth Creation

Published by:
POSAG International Ltd
9 Greenwich Quay
London
SE8 3EY

For comments or enquiries e-mail:
info@posagconsulting.com

ISBN 978-0-956468-25-3

Designed & Layout by: www.byjomedia.com

CONTENTS

PREFACE

My Life's Journey and Motivation

I was born into a family of six in the mid-1950's in Warri, Delta State, Nigeria. We lived in a mud house where there was no electricity and it was difficult to access drinkable water. My father was always in and out of menial jobs and at times, it was challenging for us to get a decent meal to eat. From an early age, I began to fend for my family by going to the waterside to collect firewood to sell. Unlike us, neighbours and friends did not have to struggle to eat, some took their access to ready available food for granted and their parents would even discipline them or buy them multivitamins when they refused to eat.

I quickly realised that knowledge was key and began to dig deep, as I wanted to satisfy my growing curiosity on the big social differences in society. Why were some living in affluence and others in abject poverty? I had tasted poverty and hated it. It was this hate that fuelled my choice to live a life dedicated to finding out exactly why the world works the way it does.

I went to college as a domestic house boy in order to fund my education because we could not afford to pay the school fees and that was the best the college could do for me. After college I went to work for Panalpina World Transportation Company in Kano state, Nigeria. I bought a house for my mother and established a

1

hotel for her. Then I bought a taxi, started a taxi firm and began to buy more vehicles, however, I was not satisfied with my level of achievement. I wanted to learn more. I wanted to become a global entrepreneur, not merely a local one. I left for the United Kingdom in 1983, where I studied accountancy. While there, I took exams to become an accountant and began to apply the knowledge I acquired to various businesses.

By 1991 I was a chartered accountant and a chartered tax advisor. As I was investing in my global education in the UK, my wife and I bought two retail shops in 1995 but had to sell them by 1999 in order to avoid bankruptcy.

In 2000, we established East London ITEC an IT and accountancy training institute. From 2001-3 I established branches of Peter Osalor and Co. throughout Nigeria, West Africa, in the following locations: Port Harcourt - River State, Warri - Delta State, Yenagoa - Bayelsa State and the city of Lagos. We truly became a multinational global enterprise. Believing I could make a difference of the state of affairs in Nigeria, I ran for governor of Delta state in 2007 but was not elected. Throughout my entire journey, I have gained extensive experience in teaching, accounting, management, capacity and business building.

Over time, I began to notice the consistent, predictable patterns and principles that appear to accompany and govern all business and career success. The most important of these principles is having an entrepreneurial attitude. This is what I aim to teach within the pages of this book. It is my desire to guide and mentor you to your path of becoming a successful entrepreneur.

My purpose in life has been the same for more than thirty years. It is to liberate the in-built potentials of individuals by giving them ideas and strategies to fast-track the benefits and rewards they can achieve as successful entrepreneurs. I intend to motivate people by making them realise that success is a choice they have to make and ANYBODY CAN BE SUCCESSFUL if they choose to be. Putting into practice my vision for entrepreneurial development in Africa, I have established several initiatives:

- I have established Success in Your Business, a UK registered charity committed to eradicating poverty by equipping individuals with the entrepreneurial spirit and the right skills to succeed in business.

- I have an on-line TV program.

- As part of my awareness creation strategy for entreprneurship, I run a weekly TV programme called Success in Your Business on African Independent Television, Abuja. A programme formerly aired on Ben TV London, GTV Ghana, NTA Warri and Port-Harcourt.

- I write a Business Blog.

- I am a regular columnist for the Vanguard Newspaper, commenting on the Nigerian economy and policy needs.

- I am a founding member of the African and Nigerian Entrepreneurs.com.

- I am a consultant to African Business Round Table on Entrepreneurship and Entrepreneurial developments.

- I have written several books on entrepreneurial success including: The Entrepreneurial Revolution: A Solution for Poverty Eradication, Why and How to Start your own Business, and How to write your Business Plan.

This book is directed at policymakers, corporate leaders, community leaders, and women who want to change women's economic position from disadvantaged to prosperous. We lay out problems emanating from women's lack of economic mobility and propose policies to improve women's economic status. We present how entrepreneurship will destroy existing barriers and provide women with viable economic enterprises. Indeed, joining the entrepreneurial revolution would reduce women's poverty and give them viable business alternatives which would feed their families and nations. Finally, we offer women a blueprint for making the entrepreneurial revolution work for them because we believe that women, who are economically empow-

ENDORSEMENT

Youth Empowerment and Entrepreneurial Revolution and Women Empowerment and Entrepreneurial Revolution by Peter Osalor – are indeed "the panacea for the youths and women who we believe have the strength and potential as well as the ability to create a change in their environments through active involvement in entrepreneurship practices." Peter Osalor, brought his experience and expertise to bear, as an Entrepreneurship Researcher, Educator and Consultant in the books, the books are practical guides towards being an entrepreneur. It is a clarion call for young men and women who will change their generations from the deadly clutches of poverty and unemployment.

The books envelope a bold, glossy and hand holding effort at stimulating the "I can do it" spirit in the Nigerian youth and women towards entrepreneurialism. That is the ability to make active positive use of their instincts, insights and perceptions to manipulate and manage them to propel them to being an entrepreneur – in spite of the obvious dangers. "You don't make an omelette without breaking an egg". It is indeed the barometer towards business ownership and management in a dynamic environment.

As the Director-General of Small and Medium Enterprises Development Agency of Nigeria (SMEDAN), I have been involved in entrepreneurship and enterprise development in Nigeria,

I therefore, see the books as "a do-it-yourself kit" that should be widely disseminated not only to youth and women, but to everybody. The books are largely an invitation to young men and women towards "being their own boss". The books are in tandem with the transformation agenda of the Mr. President, Dr. Goodluck Ebele Jonathan, GCFR, which is geared towards employment generation, wealth creation, poverty reduction and general re-prioritisation and refocusing on national delivery.

The books reenergise the spirit of creativity and innovation which drive entrepreneurship. I would like nothing more than to see these books become required reading to all who are interested in owning and managing a business enterprise, as the books have all the tools and techniques for managing a successful business enterprise. This will provide the most natural and effective prescription against all the crises this country is witnessing today, be it militancy, boko haram, communal or religious.

Muhammad Nadada Umar
Director-General/CEO
SMEDAN

ered, have better developed families and nations.

Best Wishes.

ENDORSEMENT

God has put a potential into women and it is the ability for prosperity. God has put the ability to create, multiply, nurture and grow inside of women, that is why it is the woman who multiplies one cell (seed) from the man into multiple cells called a baby. A little key, a very little key is what you need to open big doors.

Continued in this highly educative, research material are little keys to enhance the release of potentials in our womenfolk and thereby build up our services spiritually, mentally, emotionally and particularly economically.

Dr. (Mrs.) Becky Enenche (MBBS, PGDE, MNIM)
Dunamis International Gospel Centre

DEDICATION

This book 'Women Empowerment and Entrepreneurial Revolution', is a tribute to my mother and other women who share her story. My mother's name is Mrs. Eunice O. Osalor. She didn't have the opportunity to get an education because she was born a girl. Her five brothers, however, were luckier, they were sent to school because they were considered to have more prospects having being born male. At an early age of 19, she got married to Mr. George Osalor, my father who was well spoken and armed with a modern certificate-education. Despite this certification, getting and keeping a job was a big problem and in no time, the responsibility of fending for the family soon rested on her shoulders.

Being an illiterate, nonetheless, she gave herself fully into making sure that her family never lacked any good thing. She ventured into petty trading, selling everything from fruits to food stuff to clothes and any other merchandise she could lay her hands upon. Being the senior child of her own parents, Mrs. Eunice Osalor soon spread her tentacles of care towards her own brothers who, despite their educational background and military jobs, were soon relying on her for support. So despite the fact that she was denied an education, she turned out to be the 'saviour' of her family. In no distant time, her trade soon spread to other parts of the country as she penetrated the East, West, and North of Nigeria plying her trade and expanding her business horizons. I can confidently say without any shadow of doubt that I learnt my entrepreneurial skills from my mother. As a young boy, I observed her plan, strategise, and execute her business and I watched her business grow from a roadside petty trading business to a large business conglomerate that spanned the entire country.

This leaves me wondering what heights she would have attained if she had gotten an education, and had not been denied simply based on gender bias. I can only imagine what would have happened if a person like Nigeria's Ngozi Okonjo-Iweala was not given an education simply because she was born a female. Would she have had an opportunity to impact the nation and indeed the world like she is currently doing? She currently occupies the position of the 87th woman of influence in the world today owing to her aggressive pursuit of financial solutions in Nigeria and the World Bank while she was there.

ACKNOWLEDGEMENTS

To start with, I would like to thank God for enabling me make this book a reality, to Him alone be all the glory and honour. My profound thanks goes to my family, most especially my wife Mrs. Eudora Osalor who has always given me the support I have needed, every time I need it; your inestimable help is deeply appreciated. My daughter Peace Ani and her husband Chijioke Ani.

My thanks also go to Kingsley Oscar, a key member of my organisation for the relentless effort you have shown towards the production of this book, thank you so much. I would also like to thank Uju Ohiaeri for her help.

My sincere thanks also to Dr Abiodun Awomolo and Dr Hashim Gibrill both of Atlanta, USA, for their efforts in critically reviewing and helping put this book together. Mrs Ade D'Almeida for her contribution and inspiration and Pastor Matthew Ashimolowo my spiritual father and pastor, who has been a great source of inspiration in the writing of this book.

My sincere gratitude to Harry Koranteng, "my right hand man" for his time and effort.

I would also like to say thank you to Mrs. Ofueko Omogui Okaru. You sparked the interest to write this book by giving me the opportunity to embark on a training of junior staff in the FIRS, and women empowerment. During the research for the trainings, I discovered a lot and decided to put it into writing in order to effect a change.

To all my staff in London, Port-Harcourt, Warri, Yenagoa, Abuja and to Joseph and Hikmot Ademosu, I say many thanks for your support and commitment; you're all very much appreciated. Limitation of space does not permit me to individually acknowledge the innumerable number of friends and well-wishers, thank you so much.

My message to you all is that this is just the beginning; the sky can never be our limit but only our starting point. Let's keep the fire burning.

Thank you

INTRODUCTION

Women's Empowerment and Entrepreneurial Revolution
"Women hold up half the sky."

Chinese Proverb

In Zambia, a Lenje man who had many wives, stated: "women are like livestock" meaning they are priced commodities. Similarly, a Yoruba man, from Nigeria, with as many wives voiced the sentiment, "women are like hens; put them in a bullock cart and they will leave you in peace." Both statements support the second-class position women hold in society. Women constitute 70 percent of the world's 1.3 billion who live in abject poverty. The majority comprise of the oppressed, subjugated, abused, and trafficked.

In employment, they are inordinately among the ranks of the unemployed, underemployed, underpaid, and economically marginalised. They suffer economic marginalization and sometimes, invisibility as a result of an intricate web of socio-cultural biases, systemic controls, and corporate complicity.

This book, Women Empowerment and Entrepreneurial Revolution promotes an agenda for empowering women by providing them with tools to lift themselves out of poverty. Empowerment is a must for women and indeed, our world today. Without women's empowerment, we run the risk of doubling the population of the poor and stunting the growth and development of entire nations. What do we mean by empowering women? Wikipedia defines empowerment as increasing spiritual, political, social, or economic strength of individuals and communities. Likewise, the United Nations defines women's empowerment as having five components: (1) women's sense of self-worth; (2) their right to have and to determine choices; (3) their right to have access to opportunities and resources: (4) their right to have the power to control their own lives, both within and outside the home; and (5) their ability to influence the direction of social change to create a more just social and economic order, nationally and internationally.

We define women's empowerment as their ability to act on their own behalf and on their own terms in a supportive and enabling environment. Women are empowered when they can create businesses, structures, institutions, and mechanisms that improve their quality of life and that of their communities. We believe that women's empowerment is synonymous with entrepreneurial thinking.

Entrepreneurialism is an important aspect of the development of any country. Entrepreneurs are known for taking risks and opening up doors to a whole new business world. If it wasn't for entrepreneurs, we would have never discovered the benefits of the wheel, electricity and the internet, to name a few. Entrepreneurs have developed the world around us. Furthermore, it is their important contributions to society that help society grow as a whole. One of the reasons the United States is considered such a prosperous nation is because of the numerous business entrepreneurs that took their idea to the next level regardless of the risks involved.

There are several benefits to taking that risk, becoming an entrepreneur and opening up your own business venture. The freedom, the financial success and the job security are a few; however, there are also a lot of problems in entrepreneurialism including the risk factor and the chance of failure, both of which are greatly increased when the surroundings for your business are not ideal. Any business person must assess the internal and external factors that may contribute to the success or failure of their business before deciding to go through with the deal. Entrepreneurs – those businessmen and women who produce, sell, and innovate – are the backbone of modern economies. For example: China's explosive economic growth over the past 25 years is largely due to removing ownership, bureaucratic, and financial limits on the entrepreneurial drive of the Chinese people. At the heart of other rapidly growing economies such as India and Brazil are numerous small and medium scale manufacturing, retail, IT, technical, and financial firms.

In the United States, the world's biggest and most sophisticated economy, more than 60% of new jobs are created by small businesses. The US government recognises that "small business is critical to our economic recovery and strength, to building

America's future, and to helping the United States compete in today's global marketplace."

Small and medium enterprises – run according to the visions, talents, opportunities and resources of entrepreneurs – are known to bring about employment creation, provide jobs for women and youth, spread the returns of economic development, help develop rural areas, mobilise domestic savings for investment, inculcate new skills and infuse new technology, and contribute to social and political stability. Indeed, nothing short of an entrepreneurial revolution would bring women out of poverty.

Further, an entrepreneurial revolution will cause policymakers to take notice of women's economic power and harness it to stimulate growth in their economies. Whereas it is necessary to understand the importance and role of women in the development of the economies and societies in this 21st century world; most policy makers worldwide neglect the fact that women are the fastest growing economy in the world, even faster than India or China. Women are an essential part of every domain of life and are able to bring in revolutionary change. The benefits derivable from empowering women are far-reaching, starting with family advancement and moving in to national and global economic advancement. If women are empowered to do more and be more, the possibility for economic growth becomes apparent because eliminating half of a nation's workforce on the sole basis of gender has detrimental effects on the economy of that nation. It is the nation that blends the strengths of women and men that will lead the world in development (Kiyosaki 1993).

In fact, a study found that of the Fortune 500 companies, "those with more women board directors had significantly higher financial returns, including 53 percent higher returns on equity, 24 percent higher returns on sales and 67 percent higher returns on invested capital (OECD, 2008)." This study shows the impact women can have on the economy of companies. If implemented on a global scale, the inclusion of women in the formal workforce would increase the economic output of nations. Further, because economic growth and development of women results in multiplier effects on the growth of the overall society, World Bank has named the investment in women as "Smart Economics."

Indeed, entrepreneurship or investing is not an exclusive reserve of any gender. Both women and men generate the same result provided they follow the principles of investment. Kiyosaki (1993) proves with statistical data in United States, that women are better investors than men. Also, a study of National Association of Investors Corporation (NAIC), found that women- only clubs achieved average annual returns of 32% since 1951 versus 23% for men-only investment clubs. The verdict is women know how to handle money and can be greater entrepreneurs than men if the various obstacles to their development is removed or minimised

Despite the developed world's declaration that equal rights and equal opportunity are a fundamental attribute of any democratic society, despite all the progress that has been made, not just for women's rights, but for human rights; statistics indicate that the economic disparity between men and women persists. Even in the most advanced of societies, it is clear that the more prestigious and lucrative opportunities are still overwhelmingly granted to men.

Further, when opportunities are afforded to both men and women, discrimination is evident in wages as women are paid considerably less than men for the same jobs. Frequently referred to as the gender wage gap, women earn roughly 75% of men's earnings. In the corporate world, women face a glass ceiling which limits their upward mobility and are often concentrated in female ghettos or low-paying occupations. Consequently, there's danger in the perpetuated and widespread belief that women have already attained complete economic equality to men in developed societies.

The inequality of men and women is even more apparent in developing societies where women are limited in both the formal and informal sectors due to a host of factors. Those factors include a lack of education, socio-cultural biases, policy blindness, and financial constraints. These factors relegate women to the fringes of society – they work in the informal economy of trade and subsistence agriculture, lower levels of corporate employment, and invisible employment of domestic servitude.

While some exceptional women stand out who occupy sensitive and top positions in economy, politics, and society, the majority of women are underprivileged. Thus, for every President Ellen Johnson-Sirleaf of Liberia, French Chancellor, Angela Merkel, United States Secretary of State, Hilary Clinton; there are multitudes of faceless, nameless, impoverished women. Thus, the best way to fight poverty is to educate and empower women. Entrepreneurship development therefore is a crucial tool for women's economic empowerment. Entrepreneurship will give women opportunities of owning businesses, thereby increasing their personal wealth. Women's entrepreneurship will generate the needed employment in developing economies and bring in the long excluded population of women into the labor force thereby empowering them. Further, there is greater possibility that women will share their economic benefits and gains with their families, societies, and nations. According to a research study in Africa, investment in the education of women results in increasing the agricultural output and yields by 20 percent.

This book, Women Empowerment and Entrepreneurial Revolution presents a solid case for promoting entrepreneurship amongst women as a strategy for empowerment. It seeks to add to the growing body of knowledge on the characteristics of female entrepreneurs, their motivation for business ownership, and the financial and other constraints inhibiting women's participation in business. It lays out a concise economic history of women in society, biases that marginalise women, policies that militate against those biases, and what women themselves can do to empower themselves entrepreneurially. We believe that an entrepreneurial revolution (ER) will empower women and reduce poverty globally.

Chapter One

WOMEN IN THE WORLD

"When women are fully involved, the benefits can be seen immediately; families are healthier and better fed; their income savings and reinvestment go up. And what is true of families is also of communities and, in the long run, of whole countries."

Kofi Anan

Former UN Secretary General

Women own only one percent of the wealth of the world, receive ten percent share in the overall income of the world, and hold only fourteen percent of the leadership posts and offices in the public and private sectors. Apart from this, women own only one percent of the overall world's land, despite the fact they produce almost half of the overall world's food. Statistics of women in the world reveal: Women constitute almost 50% of the world's population. Women have not achieved equality with men in any country. Of the world's 1.3 billion poor people, about 70% are women.

They have lower literacy rates; over 640 million of the women in the world are illiterates. Amongst the world's children, 121 million are not in school, 60% of them are girls. Women and girls are more vulnerable to exploitation. Women's rights and access to land, credit and education are limited; not only due to legal discrimination, but due to subtle barriers such as their workload, mobility and low bargaining positions in the household and community prevent them from taking advantage of their legal rights.

Women's status/employment is outside of the formal or paid sector. 90% of the world female labour is under the umbrella of housewives and excluded from the formal definition of economic activity. Women work more unpaid hours than men. The paid ones are paid 17% lower than men. Women perform 66% of the world's work, produce 50% of the food, but earn 10% of the income and own 1% of the property.

In some regions, women provide 70% of agricultural labour, produce more than 90% of the food and yet are nowhere represented in budget deliberations.

Women occupy only 24% of senior management positions globally, 34% of which are privately held businesses. Of managerial positions, women hold 39% in developed countries, 15% in Africa, and 13% in Asia. In Arab States, only 28% of women participate in the work force. Research consistently shows that women have been the poorer sex throughout the 20th Century and have formed a substantial majority of the poor since poverty was first recognised. Indeed, the United Nations analysed the plight of women using several indicators – population, women and men in families, health, education, work, political decision making – and found that on almost every front, women were the subordinated gender.

In an attempt to measure gender disparity or the gap between males and females, the World Economic Forum conducted a study of 58 countries. They measured gender disparity in 5 areas: economic participation, economic opportunity, political empowerment, educational attainment, and health and wellbeing. Depicted in graphs, gender disparity is widest in developing regions but closer in developed ones. Different regions and countries reflect different overall performance on index of gender gap calculated by the United Nations. There are different policies and practices in different countries which, hence, have different impact on the gender gap and women economic marginalization. The graph below presents the overall ranking of different regions and the level of women marginalization in each of the regions.

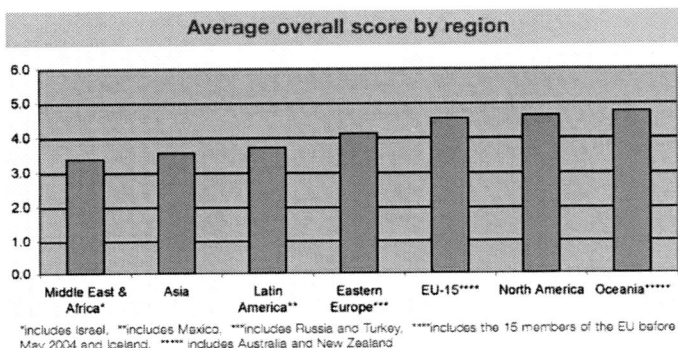

Average overall score by region

*Includes Israel. **Includes Mexico. ***Includes Russia and Turkey. ****Includes the 15 members of the EU before May 2004 and Iceland. ***** includes Australia and New Zealand

Figure 1: Regional Performance on the Overall Index of Gender Gap

Economic Participation:

The economic participation of women i.e. the number of women in the workforce of the country is an important element in order to reduce the gender gap and women's economic marginalization. Not only this, it helps in increasing the household income and in turn promoting the process of the economic growth and development. Economic participation not only covers the number of women in the labor force but is also concerned about the fact that women are paid the same pay and remuneration as men in the same positions.

24

Different regions and countries have different strategies and policies which in turn either encourage or discourage the economic participation of women. The performance of different regions on the economic participation index is shown in the graph below.

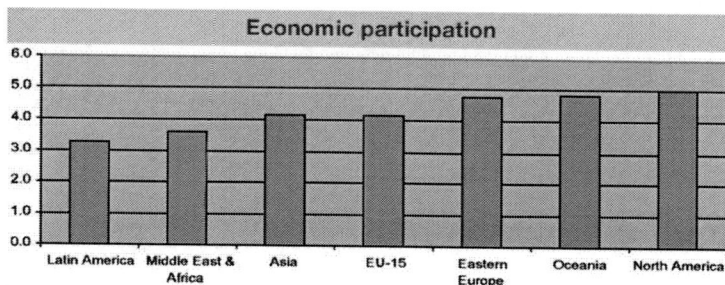

Figure 2: Regional Performance on the Economic Participation Index

Economic Opportunity:

The index of economic opportunity measures the quality of the economic involvement and jobs provided to women in different countries and regions. This means that it is not enough to only provide jobs to females but it should also be ensured that the jobs and employment provided to women are not restricted to the ones which are poorly paid. It is important to provide proper economic opportunities to women, which in turn will reduce the gender gap and women's economic marginalization. Different countries provide women with different economic opportunities and chances for economic development and growth. The performance of different regions on the index of economic opportunity is reflected in the graph below.

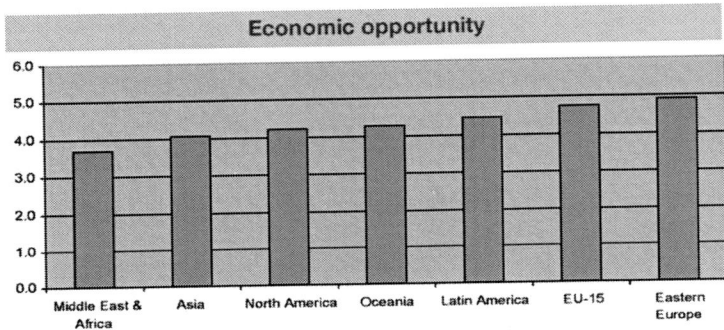

Figure 3: Regional Performance on the Index of Economic Opportunity

Political Empowerment:

In order to reduce the gender gap among males and females and to eradicate the concept of women economic marginalization it is essential to provide women with political empowerment. By providing political empowerment we mean that giving women equal representation in the decision making process and structures, either formal or informal, and that they are able to contribute in the process of policies and strategies formulation. There are very few females who have been able to reach the different levels of government. Hence the important decisions

26

related to resource allocation and other national and local policies are formulated without the participation of females who are an important constituent of the economy. The performance of the different regions on the index of political empowerment is presented in the graph below.

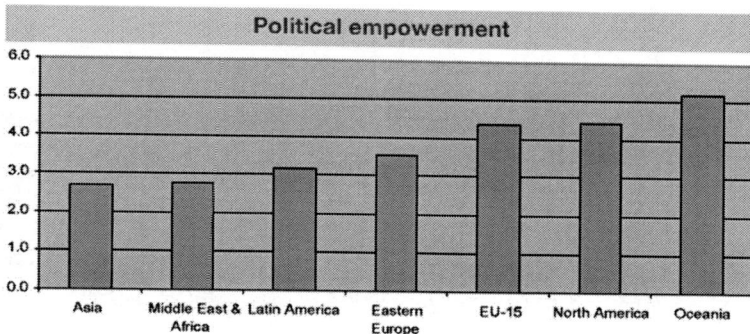

Figure 4: Regional Performance on the Index of Political Empowerment

Educational Attainment:

One of the most important dimensions of women's economic marginalization is the availability of education. Educational attainment is the most essential factor which is required in order to ensure the empowerment of women in all fields and domains. Only when females are provided with the same quality education as males, can they then compete with the males for access to well paying employment opportunities and other financial resources. Also, educational attainment is a pre-requisite for females to acquire positions and roles in the decision making process, representing government, and getting political power and influence. By improving the female literacy rate the policy makers and government can strive to eradicate women economic marginalization and empower women. The performance of different regions on the index of educational attainment is shown in the graph below.

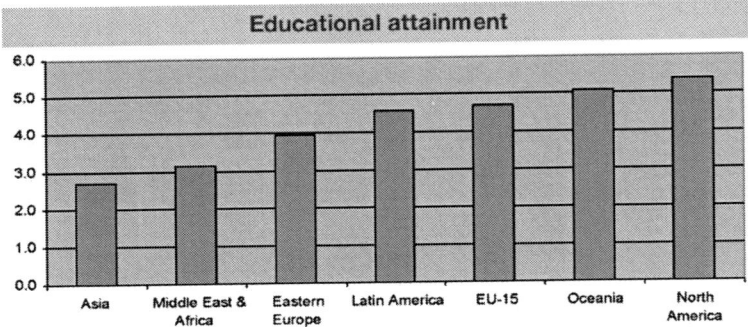

Figure 5: Regional Performance on the Index of Educational Attainment

Health and Wellbeing:

Women are not only deprived from economic participation and opportunity, political empowerment, and attainment of education but there is also a great gap between the availability of proper nutrition and food provided for females compared to males. Apart from this, women also face issues of access to healthcare facilities and safety. The World Health Organisation (WHO) reported that every year around 585,000 women die because of the issues during pregnancy and delivery.

Women are also exposed to the challenges and issues related to integrity and self-respect as they are vulnerable to violence and torture. All these contribute to the increase in the gender gap and growth of women's marginalization. The graph below presents the performance of different regions on the index of health and well-being of females.

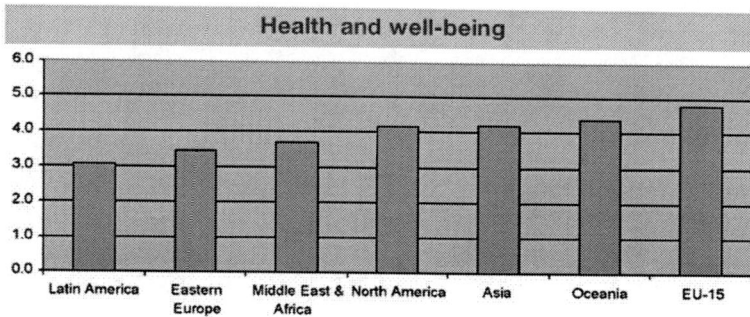

Health and well-being

Latin America	3.0
Eastern Europe	3.4
Middle East & Africa	3.7
North America	4.1
Asia	4.1
Oceania	4.1
EU-15	4.4

Figure 6: Regional Performance on the Index of Health and Well Being

Chapter Two

DIMENSIONS OF WOMEN'S ECONOMIC MARGINALIZATION

"Women often times are unheralded in the work that they do for the economies of their families, communities and even their nations. Despite the significant progress, there is still a wealth of untapped potential in women."

Yvette D. Clarke

In the pursuit of self-realisation as well as accomplishments, women have usually had to fight a little harder, stand a little taller and indeed endure a little longer so as to achieve goals in many areas, particularly in the corporate world. They are confronted with peculiar hurdles specific to their gender as women and to the sociopolitical and economic environments in which they live. Thus, gender discrimination and inequality leads to women receiving far less share in social, political, and economic power than they deserve.

This economic marginalization and inequality increases women's subordination and reduces their enjoyment of a large range of human rights. And it is not the dilemma faced by the underdeveloped or third world countries alone but also developed and modern economies. Inequalities on the basis of gender in the control of economic resources and distribution of the financial resources have resulted in placing women at a disadvantage compared to men in the process of economic development and growth.

Women's economic marginalization is revealed after comparing their economic status to men all over the world. It not only refers to their poverty level but also encompasses the economic conditions and situations women face. Researchers have shown that poverty is a malady that incapacitates its victim economically and indirectly subjects him/her to a state of destitution, voicelessness, powerlessness and even violence

(World Bank 2000; Okojie, 2002). Unfortunately, the most affected, by the above incapacitation, are women and children. Statistics show that women are poorer than men. The UNDP (2008) estimated that about 70% of the world-poor are women. This increasing proportion of poor females all over the world is recognised as the feminization of poverty, whereas women are impoverished in higher numbers than men. It calculates the number of women who live below the poverty line as heads of households; girls placed in domestic servitude, early marriages and sex trafficked around the world, and females caught in the crossfire of wars either internally displaced or in refugee camps. Different factors contribute to the feminization of poverty. They include: policy biases towards males, socio-cultural biases, corporate marginalization, victimisation from war, family status and lack of educational opportunities and skills development.

Policy biases

A major contributor to women's economic marginalization is the fact that planners of the economic development process are mostly or entirely men who include women in the process only in the roles of mothers, sisters, daughters, and wives but not as individuals in their own rights. Women have been provided with limited opportunity to participate in or contribute to the economic decision making process. The female/male ratio within parliament in a large number of nations remains a great concern in Western Democracy.

In the European parliament for instance almost 2/3 of them are male, although this has increased 16% to 24% from 1997 to 2009, but nevertheless the female demographic is still notably under represented. In national governments, the situation is improving steadily with the share of women senior ministers in EU governments at 27%. The European Commission counts nine women Commissioners (33%) and eighteen men (67%), the best gender balance yet – up from 5.6% in 1994/1995.

In the United States of America, only 2% of the CEOs from Fortune 500 companies are female. And in the OECD countries, women represent only 7% of the director positions of leading and top companies. Similarly, there are no women on the boards of over 46% of top companies in OECD countries and only 23% of the companies have more than one woman on the company board. In United States of America, only 13% of the board members are women, whereas in Canada this percentage is as low as 11%. According to the statistics of European Commission, central banks of the countries in the European Union only have male governors and women only represent about 17% of the main decision making units within the companies of these countries.

A factor responsible for the pro-male bias of policies is that there are too few women in the policymaking arena. For example, according to the Nigerian Minister of Women Affairs and Social Development, the latest Nigerian census revealed that women constitute 49.9% of the nation's population but only 2% of the policymakers. The underrepresentation of women in the nation's development processes in finance, business and investment fronts renders 40% of the population inadequately positioned to contribute to the economic growth of the country. Alongside, women who seek fair political representation face serious opposition and criticism.

Socio-cultural Biases

To many people, it just seems natural that women are worse off because of their smaller size or their capacity to bear children. Men comfort themselves with the thought that women need looking after. Hence, from the very beginning, women have been perceived as a weaker gender in all societies and were not provided with equal opportunities. Today, women are still not considered equal to men and are subjected to violence and abuse, and provided with less economic, educational, political, and health care opportunities.

Lingering nuclear family ideals, which many people are still conditioned to believe is "natural", may play a part in deterring women from pursuing economic sovereignty - but also perhaps in deterring men from granting those opportunities to women. In the nuclear family, gender roles are thus defined: men are expected to be the primary breadwinners and women are expected to be nurturers that look after children and the family as a whole. In the western world, females are legally of equal status to males; they have equal access to education, as well as all other services and amenities. But there are subtle and more discreet forms of discrimination and prejudice when it comes to granting more opportunities to women.

Males are still not only expected to be the primary breadwinner, but under pressure to make more money than their spouses or risk appearing inadequate or unable to provide. In other words, conventional nuclear family gender roles are still viewed to be the norm and they hurt women's chances of economic mobility outside of the nuclear family. To state on the one hand that men are the primary breadwinners and on the other hand that women can go earn as much as they can, is confusing. And this confusion creates the continuing subordination of women's economic goals and aspirations to society's ideals of gender roles thus, the gender gap persists.

What persists in society translates into underemployment for women whereas an employer may assume that a woman does not want a higher level position or the stress that comes with it or a female employee will likely take pregnancy leave in the future or when married or she may decide to leave her job all together. Hence, women are offered "temporary" positions or non-career paths that don't offer opportunities for upward mobility.

Corporate Marginalization

Corporate marginalization describes the lower and immobile positions women hold in the corporate world. There are various factors which account for women's corporate marginalization and the increasing difference in the economic condition of working women in comparison with men. Some of the crucial factors are:

- **Pay inequity**
- **Glass ceiling**
- **Placement in Female Ghettos**
- **Work and family balance**

Pay Inequity

Women form one third of the overall formal labor force of the world. Despite this fact, most of their work remains unpaid. In many developing countries, women work longer hours than men by over 30% but the male employees receive higher wages compared to the female employees. The wage rate of women in different countries is around 50% less than that of men; for example in Georgia, the average earnings of women is around 40% of the average earnings of men.

In 2004 the median income for full time workers was $40,798 for males, compared to $31,223 for females. So in 2004, women's wages were 76.5% of men's wages. This however does not take into account differences in experience, skill, occupation, education or hours worked, as long as the hours of work qualify as full time work, meaning anything upwards of thirty hours. Indeed, the International Trade Union Confederation estimated that the earnings of women across the globe are 16.5% less than men.

Until the 1950s in the United States, men and women working side by side, doing exactly the same job were paid different wages. This was not a secret. "Help Wanted" ads actually listed "men's rates" and "women's rates". This was prior to the civil rights movement and the equal pay acts of 1963, in the states, and the subsequent acts of other western nations, who followed suit. As significant and effective as this act was, it's initial impact on women was overestimated, this was believed to be the solution to the problem, the end of the economic disparity, however this was just one small step towards women's economic sovereignty. The act demanded equal pay for equal work.
It was a necessary step forward, certainly in the right direction and certainly beneficial to women, but it was merely a scratch on the surface of what was a much more deeply rooted problem. In addition to low wages, women are unemployed for longer periods. For example, in the Republic of Moldova 68 % of the unemployed are females and in Armenia this percentage is around 66%. The difference in pay also reduces women's decision making authority. They are provided with little opportunity to hold decision-making positions or offices. There are only 10% to 30%

of women managers in the private sector in most countries and around 5% of the top positions are occupied by females. Also, women or female employees are not given due representation in the trade unions or any other such movements.

Glass Ceiling

Glass ceiling describes the barriers faced by most of the women who aim to reach the position or office of leadership or top management. These women start climbing the corporate ladder desiring to become CEO one day, but halfway up, they stop getting promotions and their climb to the top stops short.

The hierarchy of most corporations is dominated by males who through old boys' networks, gender biased expectations, and sexual harassment create serious challenges and hurdles to the progress of the females. These practices stop women's professional growth and development despite all the education, skills, and experience they bring to the organisations.

Further, women who are able to reach the leadership positions are exposed to a second type of glass ceiling, as reflected by a study of managers in multi-national organisations these women were able to hold the high management office and were given the same pay and bonuses as male managers, but were managing less staff, had fewer stock options, and were provided with very little overseas and important projects. Having the same job title or position does not mean that the people in both positions have the same status level. Women were restricted from exploring further growth opportunities.

Placement in Female Ghettos

The term, "female ghetto" describes jobs which are low paying because of the high concentration of women such as farming, teaching, nursing, and social work. History tells us that women have always been contributing to the agriculture sectors around the world and despite of much advancement this trend has not changed even today, as a major portion of women are still employed in this sector. According to the International Labor Organisation the percentage of women working in agriculture sector around the world is 35.4% whereas the ratio of men in this sector is 32.2%. This ratio further increases in sub-Saharan Africa and South Asian regions as more than 60% are employed in the agriculture sectors of all female employment.

Even when they work in progressive fields, women tend to be concentrated on the lower ranks of the industry. For example, the ratio of women working in the domain of computer programming and other related fields comprise only 20% to 30% in countries like China, Germany, USA, France and the Republic of Korea and up to about 70% in Ghana. However, most of them are employed at lower level positions like data entry operator, telemarketing representatives and call centre agents.

Alternative explanations for "female ghettos" are that jobs typically suited to males simply pay more than those typically intended for females because they are generally more physically taxing and are of a higher personal risk. Also men are more likely to choose jobs simply because they pay more, whereas women are more concerned with flexible hours and what the job itself entails.

Work and Family Balance

From the very start, females are perceived to be responsible for taking care of household chores and activities. According to different studies the working hours of women are longer than men all over the world. However, most of the work done by women is unpaid domestic work. Women who have full time employment outside their homes still perform most of the household responsibilities. In order to reduce the extent of women's economic marginalization, it is important to create a balance between work and family life.

Most women, if given the opportunity, would work from home or in an environment where they can care for their children. Thus they choose jobs with more flexible hours, or hours complementary to their childcare needs such as teaching, trade, farming, childcare work, etc. Men on the other hand have no familial constraints and thus tend to work more hours and choose jobs that are typically higher paying.

War

In the developing world, the most crucial factor contributing towards the increasing marginalization of women is ongoing war. It has been estimated that about 90% of the total casualties of war are civilians and out of this percentage, 80% of the casualties are women and children. Women become impoverished as they lose or bury breadwinner husbands and flee homes, stable jobs, and support systems due to war. Instead, they head on to refugee camps where they experience economic stagnation, unemployment, and poverty.

Family Status

Divorce, widowhood, and single parenting can create instant poverty for women. Indeed, it is said that divorce causes most women and their children to immediately fall below the poverty line. For example, in 2001 in the U.S., out of the 32.9 million people living in poverty around 52% were women, and at the same time 49% of those families living below the poverty line were headed by single females.

Lack of Educational Opportunities and Skills Development

One of the major factors that undergird discrimination against women in the labor market in different parts of the world is the lack of/limited educational opportunities provided to women.

According to UNESCO in 2006, the share of women in scientific tertiary studies was only 29% and 16% in the field of engineering.

Challenges to Female Entrepreneurship

Organisations such as the World Bank have pointed out that progress is slow with regards to improving women's economic opportunities. For instance, in low income countries women consistently trail men with regards to their access to credit, the amount of credit, entrepreneurship rates, income levels, and inheritance and ownership rights. While economic equality has at least to some degree been attained in the west, the valued economic opportunities are still being overwhelmingly granted to men. Men are still the CEOs, the Executives, the owners of capital and more heavily represented in parliament, meaning only their ideas and ideals are being expressed.

When looking at which demographics more frequently hold the majority of power and wealth, it becomes clear that women have only attained economic equality at a very fundamental level. The business setting for women, which reflects a multifarious relationship between the diverse hindering factors earlier stated ultimately results in the disadvantaged status of women in the society, and as a result, women lag behind their male counterparts. For example, the reality of the situation in many African and other transitional economies is that female entrepreneurs consistently struggle to succeed yet remain dormant (Nichter and Goldmark, 2009). According to Brush (1992) finance for business start-up represents the biggest obstacle for female entrepreneurs, as many women are seen to commence their business activities with lower levels of finance compared to their male counter-parts. This has been argued to be the main problem militating against their establishment and growth.

Women entrepreneurs around the world generally face more barriers to obtain finance for their projects than men entrepreneurs and this is the reason why there are fewer women entrepreneurs. In South Africa, for example, the ratio of women is only 5% of the total clients of a black economic empowerment equity fund of a major bank after two years of its operations. The situation in Bangladesh is even worse as the deposits by women comprise only 27% of the total deposits whereas the ratio of women taking credit was only 1.8%. Also loans of businesses led by women in Bangladesh are less than 2% in the country. In Uganda, the ratio of women taking loans for businesses is only 9% which further declines in rural areas to 1%. The evidence suggests that female entrepreneurs have greater difficulty gaining access to relevant financial resources needed to successfully launch a new venture or grow an existing business. An explanation for this could be because financial institutions are often perceived as lending to the person and not the business per say. And as women are considered secondary earners, their creditworthiness is questionable.

Further, female entrepreneurial firms are relatively young compared to their male counterparts; they have no track record and are inexperienced. In addition, many women originate from low paid employment and unemployment, and as such lack savings or collateral for external financing (Riding and Swift, 1990). This unavailability of adequate finance for fixed assets and working capital is a dire problem facing female entrepreneurs in Africa despite the various sources from which small to medium sized Enterprises can access credit (Brush et al., 2001, 2002; DTI, 2005). Because of limited access to capital, a high percentage of women start their firms with their own savings or support from family and friends. This is sometimes supplemented by short-term credit offered by suppliers and advances from buyers. They are also observed to resort to traditional banking sources to meet their capital requirements (Anna et al., 1999; DTI, 2005).

The condition of female entrepreneurs is also compounded by the following factors:

- Financial Constraints: by far the most challenging of the problems entrepreneurial women face, lack of access to capital determines the enterprises they pursue, the size of their businesses, opportunities for expansion, and revenue generated.

- Lack of Infrastructural Facility for workspace and business premises: due to age old practices of excluding women from inheritance; women have fewer land holdings than men on which to build their businesses. They also may lack collateral to request large loans for infrastructural development.

- Lack of Assets: women face barriers when trying to obtain loans from traditional banks because of a lack of assets to use as collateral. This factor also limits there opportunities for expansion hence their businesses are small.

- Social Environment: in environments rife with gender biased practices such as sexual harassment, women often feel intimidated. They shy away from pursuing certain types of projects or more lucrative contracts because of a fear of harassment. Cultural and Family Responsibilities: familial obligations often limit the options women can pursue in business. Taking this into consideration, we have devoted a chapter in this book to review home-based opportunities women may pursue.

- Access to Training: women may be untrained for new business opportunities such as those in the technology industry. While trade and farming are traditional, there's need to increase women's earning capacity to embrace new frontiers. Competition: women are often on unequal footing when they compete with men for contracts or business opportunities. They are often less educated, funded, and experienced.

Also, if they run into an old boys' network, they are over-powered.

- Tax Burden: while both male and female entrepreneurs recognise taxation as a heavy burden, women feel a heavier burden because their enterprises are smaller. As a result, they are less likely to register their businesses than men. For example, Rwandan women entrepreneurs register 22.3 % of businesses while men register 27.6 %.

Chapter Three

COSTS OF WOMEN'S ECONOMIC MARGINALIZATION
TO GLOBAL ECONOMY

"The current way companies appeal to women is to take a male product and paint it pink."

Michael Silverstein,

A partner at Boston Consulting Group (BCG)

It is disheartening to see that only one in ten board members of Europe's largest companies are female and all central bank governors are male. Male CEOs and Entrepreneurs still far outnumber females, and in politics women are still severely underrepresented. Interestingly, numerous organisations and countries have come to acknowledge the costs of women's marginalization to their economies. These costs include: persistent underdevelopment, economic stagnation and decline, corporate disorientation, loss of potential workforce, lower standards of living both in households and communities, and even poorer health and environmental qualities.

According to the European Union (EU), the key to economic growth and repairing the economic damage that has been done to the global economy is to elevate women to more prestigious positions. This need for more women in positions of power transcends the mere principle of equality, but is one of economic necessity. For example, studies show that companies where women are well represented are also better off financially. Thus, it goes beyond merely nurturing the female demographic, although that's important as well. The incentive for companies and for nations is improved economic stability. Further, several studies reveal that gender diversity pays off and that there is a positive correlation between the share of women in senior positions and company performance. For example, a study conducted in Finland found that firms with a gender-balanced board are on average 10% more profitable than those with an all-male board.

According to a study conducted under the Swedish EU Presidency in 2009, eliminating gender gaps in employment in the EU Member States could lead to a potential 15% - 45% increase in GDP. Measures to improve gender imbalances can benefit the decision making process. Such measures that have been put forth are equality plans, the defining of targets and monitoring of the progress, better provisions for work-life balance, the promotion of female role models, mentoring programs and networking.

Policy makers and government officials neglect and ignore the fastest growing segment of several economies at great cost. Their ignorance and negligence is resulting in increasing the problem of women economic marginalization. This phenomenon of women's economic marginalization has serious implications, drawbacks, and high costs. These implications and drawbacks can be divided into two different types in order to better understand the impact of women's economic marginalization; one is the direct influence on the women and their families and second is the more broad influence on the economy and society.

Women's increasing economic marginalization restricts the process of economic growth and development. Women can play important roles in the development of the economy and society if provided with proper opportunities and chances.

In order to avoid all the negative impact and effect of women's economic marginalization, it is necessary to recognise the importance of females and stop treating them as third world citizens. Top companies are neglecting and ignoring this major sector of the market. The financial services institutions are the biggest offender in this regard. According to the survey by the Boston Consulting Group, the organisations which offer financial services like i-banking, insurance, investment and others have the worst record of dealing with their female clients.

Their neglect results in loss of potential clients and a growing market share. They would do better packaging financial services that meet the unique needs of female entrepreneurs. In Nigeria for example, women's participation and role within the wider entrepreneurial setting is constantly undermined, resulting in the gross underestimation of women's socioeconomic contribution to the economy and underutilization of women's tremendous potentials (Woldie and Adersua, 2004). Furthermore, female entrepreneurs in Nigeria are faced with a myriad of obstacles and challenges, and the lack of support from government and non-governmental agencies further exasperates their effort. Many women in Africa and in Nigeria have been forced into alternative avenues of generating income, with a greater number of women setting up in business as a result of chronic poverty, corporate glass ceilings and high unemployment (Madichie, 2009). Unfortunately, as entrepreneurs, women face a different set of constraints further compounded by the need to compete in an aggressive business environment with rapidly changing technologies and the globalisation of production, trade, and financial flows (UNIDO, 2001). This is also in addition to their double shifts as wives, mothers and business women which are intricate for female entrepreneurs in a developing or transitional economy (Woldie and Adersua, 2004). Consequently, female entrepreneurs in many societies are exhorted to be both producers and reproducers, bearing the dual burden of full-time work and domestic responsibilities (Goscilo, 1997).

The World Bank asserts that not investing in women actually limits economic growth and slows poverty reduction. In other words countries with greater gender equality tend to have lower poverty rates. Gender equality is simply put, smart economics. So what the World Bank has done to help bolster women's economic opportunities and speed implementation has been called the "gender mainstreaming strategy". They also launched Gender Equality as Smart economics or (GAP), a four year action plan with resources from the banks own funds, coupled with donated contributions at $63 million dollars. Key donors include the governments of Australia, Canada, Denmark, Germany, Iceland, Norway, Spain, Sweden, Italy, and the United Kingdom. Through competitive calls for proposals, the GAP is now funding 195 World Bank projects, and analytical work focusing on the GAP's target sectors in more than 73 countries.

In April 2008, Bank President Robert B. Zoellick committed the Bank to new measures to boost women's economic empowerment. By 2010, at least half of the bank's rural and agricultural products will address a gender concern, expected to total US$800 million; the World Bank Group will channel at least US$100 million through the IFC towards women entrepreneurs by 2012, The International Development Association (IDA) will increase investments for gender equality and Innovative engagements with foundations and the private sector will help boost women's economic empowerment. In addition to this, IFC increased its credit lines for women entrepreneurs through five commercial banks in 12 countries by US$48 million.

It is perceived that the economic marginalization and inequality among males and females results in increasing female crime rate. The gender gap in crime has reduced with the passage of time. More and more females are indulging in criminal activities and it is believed that this reduction in the gender gap in crime is directly related with the increase of the financial instability of females and growing women economic marginalization. Organisations today, perhaps most notably the World Bank and UNIFEM, have introduced legislation not just because it is fundamentally the right thing to do, but because it is economically vital to economic growth and repair. The reality is investing in women benefits everyone. Evidence indicates that an increase in women's income will lead to improvements in child health, nutrition and education.

Chapter Four

POLICIES AND PROGRAMS THAT EMPOWER WOMEN
AND WHAT GOVERNMENTS CAN DO

*"Nations in South Asia and Africa lose .5 to 1 percent growth
per-capita income per year compared to similar countries
where children have greater access to quality, basic education."*

The World Bank

In much of the Western world, there have been significant policies enacted to reduce the gender gap and to address women's economic marginalization. On such measure is the equal work for equal pay, also known as the equal pay act which was the first and no doubt the most pivotal measure enacted. Starting in America, it demonstrated the government's and society's intentions to remove systematic gender oppression and to facilitate women's economic independence. Now, a female driving a forklift would receive the same payment as a male operating a forklift, given they both have equal experience.

Also now women could work such jobs, where as previously there were only a select few jobs women could perform. The catalyst for gender equality and the most important measure initiated the movement to close the gender gap was the equal pay act legislated in 1963. The rest of Western world soon followed suit introducing their own versions of the equal pay act, which essentially made it illegal to pay females who were doing the same job as males less money, equal pay for equal work was the underlying principle of the act. The equal pay act was part of a new frontier program. In passing the bill the goal was to denounce discrimination based on sex.

What pay equity does is ensure that jobs are paid based on their relative value to society. So for instance a Nurse, typically a female orientated occupation, highly valued to society should be paid the same amount as say, an electrician, a typical male orientated job, whose value to society to a nurse is comparable. So females can continue to work their preferred jobs and still be compensated for according to the worth of that job. What this legislation does is address a problem that lingers as a result of systematic economic discrimination, not individual discrimination. The UK and Australian governments have similar legislation as does most of the Western world. Australia's old centralised wage fixing system, "equal pay for work of equal value" by women was introduced in 1969. Anti-discrimination on the basis of sex was legislated in 1984. The UK passed their equal pay act in 1970 to prevent discrimination on terms of employment between men and women, and a similar act in France in 1972.

Female orientated work tends to be more social, they're typically government jobs or jobs in the service industry. If this disparity between female and male orientated professions is not dealt with, female work will continue to be undervalued and underpaid. What the pay equity laws do is assert a more proactive role and require employers to examine the pay systems and eliminate discrimination in wages. This policy is effective because it addresses the two different umbrellas under which females and males typically work and levels them out accordingly. It acknowledges wage discrimination as systematic discrimination, not individual discrimination, which is what the first act failed to recognise.

For instance if a female decides to work as a social worker who earns $30,000 and both males and females are paid the same for this job but only one of ten social workers are in fact male, but the male equivalent to this job is say plumbing or construction which rakes in up to $70,000 and nine out of ten plumbers are male, you haven't really addressed the main source of the problem. The entire demographic is being discriminated against, not individuals. What this legislation does is force organisations to level them out. Although it was not known at the time, this wasn't enough to completely remove the economic disparity between the genders. It took roughly 19 years after this measure was put in place for the American government to discover that the gender gap had not been completely corrected, after which organisations began to form to combat what was evidently a much more complicated problem.

In January 2009, as part of the objective to foster public-private partnerships for women's empowerment, the World Bank also launched a Private Sector Leaders Forum at the World Economic Forum in Davos. The World Bank's GAP program also complements the IFC's Gender Entrepreneurship Market's work in establishing lines of credit for female bankers and entrepreneurs. GAP funds training for commercial bank staff, to better serve their female customers and women entrepreneurs and to enhance financial literacy and management skills. In Tanzania, an IFC credit line of US$5 million resulted in loans to 10 small and medium enterprises, and to 'Sero Lease', a woman-owned micro-leasing company, with an outreach to 30,000 women. While the overall impact of such programs and measure remains to be seen, progress is being made and money is being allocated in the right areas. The World Bank is leading the way and is targeting the source of remaining economic disparity, lack of women in positions of power, authority and influence, as well as the social mores still prevalent in developed countries.

The United Nations has also been right up there alongside the World Bank. The United Nations created a development fund for women (UNIFEM), which was established as a separate fund within the United Nations development program (UNDP) in 1984, with the intention of promoting women's involvement in mainstream activities. The purpose initially was to facilitate and encourage female participation and perspective on legal, social and political institutions to policy development, the research, planning, advocacy and development. UNIFEM wanted to ensure that the female gender was not merely an accompanying perspective but rather as significant as a male's perspective. UNIFEM was critical at bringing significant attention to a prevailing injustice which was believed to have been corrected by the legislations initiated by developed nations.

Organisations such as the ICRW and the World economic forum, whose efforts are directed exclusively towards improving not only women's economic empowerment but women's status, provide critical research, statistics and updates on the relative effectiveness of globally implemented programs. They also provide suggestions and strategies through their analysis of data. These organisations play a role in determining where larger, more wealthy organisations can best put their money, so the most pressing and detrimental issues can be corrected first, thereby maximising their money's effectiveness.

Despite the marginalization of the majority of women, there are several success stories of female entrepreneurs and leaders in all domains of life. There have been different successful women not only in the business sector but also in politics and other sectors of life. Women are the largest emerging economic force which is demanding attention and consideration of policy makers all over the world to construct and promote better policies for the economic well fare and well being of women. The economic development is directly related to the advancement and growth of women. According to Verheul et al. (2006), female entrepreneurs are now considered important forces in economic development of their nations. This does not come as a surprise because in very recent times, due to the state of the economy over the world, women have been forced to venture into business and other sources of income generation in order to cope with the demands and commitments to the home.

For example, Welter et al (2006) notes that "Women in business are a growing force in the economy, and in transition environment, their contribution extends from the economic sphere to include the wider process of social transformation" (Welter et al., 2006: 3).

A UNIDO report on Africa also acknowledges this trend as women were reported to be in charge of the majority of activities in Africa (UNIDO, 2008). This finding is also reflected in various studies which indicate that women, own and operate around one-third of all businesses in the formal sector, and they represent the majority of businesses in the informal sector (Bardasi et al., 2007; World Bank, 2007; Aderemi et al., 2008).

The work of the United Nations and many other agencies in advancing gender equality has converged, it is clear that there are three areas which need to be focused on: 1) Strengthening women's economic capacity, i.e. increasing the amount of credit available to women at an entrepreneurial and corporate level, extending economic power to women in third world countries where the economic disparity is much greater 2) Promoting women's leadership and political participation, in many developed countries where basic gender equality appears to have been achieved, the battlefront has shifted to removing the more intangible discrimination against working women.

In these areas, the concentration is on eliminating violence against women and supporting the implementation of the Convention on the Elimination of Discrimination against Women (CEDAW). Eventually the pay equity acts and equal pay acts may be implemented in developing nations to eliminate the economic disparity when those nations have undergone, to put it bluntly, a change of attitudes towards the female demographic. One of the countries on the leading edge of change in this regard is Rwanda where women have gained majority seats in the parliament. Stemming from this and greater opportunities for women to make a difference in Rwandan economy, the government, Chamber of Commerce, and private sectors have doubled their efforts to ensure that women can fully participate in the rebuilding of the Rwandan economy.

Other countries in Sub-Saharan Africa would do well to undertake the following:

Ways to Empower Women for Entrepreneurship Development

- Introducing legal reforms to ensure equal rights of women to ownership, inheritance and financial control; with a view to reinforcing their special skills and advantages and leveraging them for immediate and long-term macro-economic gains, at both local and national levels.

- Re-prioritising budgetary outlays and official expenditure models with the specific objective of improving gender equality, through the introduction of special schemes and programmes that effectively encourage women's involvement in entrepreneurial activities.

- Enforcing equitable gender participation through the development of focused entrepreneurial activity for women that takes their socio-cultural, legal, and economic constraints into account. Policy changes must be initiated to overcome hurdles in the gainful involvement of women in viable enterprises.

- Initiating government incentive programmes for existing and emerging enterprises that proactively involve women in different hierarchies. Educating present and future entrepreneurs on the unique business and social advantages they stand to derive from this dynamic group.

- Facilitating partnerships between women and financial advisory and support agencies; in a way that compensates their lack of formal business acumen, experience and access to funding. Fostering partnerships between women entrepreneurs in related sectors to help share expertise and resources.

- Instituting effective start-up and ongoing support structures with safety net provisions to provide continuous financial, technical and know-how assistance and minimise failure rates. Ensuring ground level efficacy of such measure through continuous monitoring and surveys.

- Enhancing accountability on women empowerment issues at both state and federal government levels through unbiased assessment of executive agencies and relevant state-sponsored programmes. Suitably highlighting achievements and deficiencies to enable constructive evolution of such practices.

- The complementary policy issues in entrepreneurship education should include increasing women enrolment in schools at all levels especially in the field of agriculture to reduce gender inequality. Budgetary allocation should be made to accommodate more continuing and vocational education.

- More seminars/workshops should be sponsored and extended to rural areas to increase women's capacity to start and grow their agribusiness, prepare sound business plans/feasibility studies and increase their technical and managerial capacity in agribusiness.

- Modern processing plants/storage facilities should be installed for women groups on government/private joint partnership basis so that women can process and store farm produce with ease.

- Creating an enabling environment in terms of gender-friendly policies, good roads, pipe-borne water and electricity should be provided by the various arms of government.

- Cooperatives and women groups should be more formally instituted and encouraged among women to position them strategically to access funds and other inputs with ease.

- The government should mandate the commercial Banks to produce more gender-friendly loan packages (low interest rates and more relaxed duration of repayment).

- Women should be exposed to the latest agro-technology from time-time to remove drudgery in farming, processing and preservation techniques.

- Women should be encouraged to network more, both at national and international levels for more exposure, to access funds and export information.

- Agro-extensions institutions should be boosted and more women extension agents be trained to reduce women to extension workers ratio and for wider coverage of women agriculturists.

- The government and development/change agencies must not only be prepared to recognise the economic role of the women but must also extend to them the same recognition and facilities as the men are enjoying.

Chapter Five

POVERTY ERADICATION AND ENTERPRENEURIAL
REVOLUTION: THE WAY FORWARD

*"Global markets and women are not often used in the same
sentence, but increasingly, statistics show that women have economic clout—most visibly as entrepreneurs and most powerfully
as consumers."*

Irene Natividad,

1998 Summit Director, Fifth Global Summit of Women and Chairwoman

Entrepreneurial revolution is the answer for change in Africa and indeed the developing world. Entrepreneurship will reduce dependence on government funding as businesses will be able to provide products and services for their nations. Given an entrepreneurial mindset, even those in government will benefit from more efficient services. Further, more tax revenue will flow into the government, allowing for more opportunities to be created and programs implemented that will work on reducing poverty rates. Businesses will also create jobs as they hire employees.

If Nigeria and other African and developing countries are to bring about an entrepreneurial revolution, they must know that it involves committed participants; resources; policy innovation and persistence; leadership; and publicity to win public support. The analysis presented in this book has made clear that if the majority of African women who form the crux of those living below the poverty line are to be lifted out of poverty, governments and individuals must commit to the entrepreneurial revolution. As Obadina, a prominent political economist notes:

African countries have stocks of raw entrepreneurial talent in small and medium scale enterprises which with training, technology and a supportive political environment, can evolve into capable managers and successful industrialists able to compete globally.

Also as President Kagame declared, "entrepreneurship is the surest way" for Rwanda and Africa to develop. Africa has the natural resources, the human resources, and the pressing need for this revolution. Just as has been the case in China, India, Brazil, and across Asia, and Latin America, a thoroughgoing entrepreneurial revolution is what will bring millions of people out of the cycle of poverty in Africa. Wishful and fuzzy thinking and relying on handouts will not get the continent anywhere. If it is to achieve the entrepreneurial revolution, it must develop the mindset, and the enabling environment for enterprise growth. It must move beyond an economy based largely on subsistence farming, subsistence enterprise, and the export of raw materials.

We must grow and diversify the African economy, just like the Asian economy, and increasingly the economies of Latin America and Central Europe. We must shape a future where African economy is producing capital and consumer goods and providing services for our own markets and the global market. Just as the world sells a broad range of available goods and services to us, so we must sell to the world.

There is no other way if we are to alleviate poverty and realise our potential as individuals, nations and a continent. We must realise that we are our own liberators. We can seek assistance from others in terms of inspiration, models, and funds, but we must find our own way, and take control of our own destiny. What will bring about and sustain the entrepreneurial revolution is individual passion and drive, and government support and facilitation of entrepreneurship. Individuals must envision and then pursue their entrepreneurial future. Governments must shape a conducive business environment in terms of infrastructure, the legal framework, financial assistance, and vocational and technical education.

As stated in the introduction, women's empowerment is women's ability to act on their own behalf and on their own terms in a supportive and enabling environment. They are empowered when they can create businesses, structures, institutions, and mechanisms that improve their quality of life and those of their communities. An entrepreneurial revolution provides a mechanism for empowerment which would bring women out of poverty. By starting their own businesses in an enabling and supportive environment, women are empowered and able to empower their communities.

Though empowerment goes beyond simply being able to start or maintain one's own business, we focus on entrepreneurship because it has been shown over time to be an activity that liberates women to pursue their own empowerment. We define entrepreneurship as the use of one's talents, skills, and ideas to serve the needs of others for monetary gain. That is, an entrepreneur generates revenue by initiating, building, and maintaining a business enterprise. Similarly, an entrepreneurial revolution is a boom of entrepreneurial initiatives and an entrepreneurial way of thinking facilitated by a collaborative and supportive environment. The revolution would promote rapid and sustainable economic expansion with specific focus on unique and creatively evolved business models. Governments can create supportive environments in which women are able to start and maintain viable businesses. A great example of this type of business climate is evolving in Rwanda. In this country one observes that the government is working hard to create an entrepreneurial environment which would serve as a catalyst to the nation's economic growth.

In the 'Ease of Doing Business' category of the World Bank, Rwanda which had ranked #143 leapt into the 67th position. It also ranked amongst the 10 most-improved economies in the world! What Rwanda has done is nothing short of miraculous given that both its political and economic lives had been devastated by the genocide of the 1990s! It had suffered human resource shortage, infrastructural damage, and ethno cultural imbroglio. Yet, several positive manifestations occurred as a result of its crisis-ridden state.

First, women gained the majority in parliament and made the country the first in the world to have a female-dominated parliament. Consequently, these women began to propose policies that were more gender inclusive and began the laborious task of healing their country after the devastating genocide of the 1990s. Women have made great strides in terms of starting new businesses alone or in partnership and their labor force participation rate is at 80%. Women's productive activity, particularly in industry empowers them economically and enables them to contribute significantly to overall development. Indeed, women head 42% of enterprises and comprise 58% of enterprises in the informal sector which accounts for 30% of Rwandan GDP.

The Rwandan example underscores the need for an entrepreneurial revolution globally and especially in Sub-Saharan Africa. In fact, enhancing entrepreneurial activities in Africa is a decisive element of poverty eradication strategy. For example, a look into Nigeria's recent past paints a picture of a country that is yet to live up to its potential. Despite high expectations that heralded Nigeria's independence, everything that's happened since seems to spiral downwards as the years rolled by and the governments changed.

In the beginning when Nigeria was basking in the euphoria of independence with agriculture as her mainstay, terms such as food imports were uncommon. The country had enough to feed her population and still export some. Agricultural wonders such as the groundnut pyramids in Kano were normal sights to behold. But with the discovery of oil in the early 1970s, decline in agricultural production ensued. The boom in the oil sector enticed youth away from the land and into the urban landscapes all wanting to land white collar jobs in either the private or public sector. Government officials became laid back as everyone waited for 'free' money from oil before they could carry out their responsibilities. This led to the death of the agricultural sector. As a result, food production did not keep up with increasing population and Nigeria began to import food. As the drive for greener pastures increased following the oil boom, more people flooded into the urban areas and soon there weren't enough jobs to go around. Things further deteriorated to 20% unemployment of about 30 million. This figure didn't include the 40 million youth captured in World Bank statistics for 2009. Similarly, UNICEF's survey indicates that about 71% of Nigerians live below the poverty line; 36% of these are the core poor while 31% are moderately poor. And these percentages are rising as there are precious few programs targeting the demographics.

The need for a wakeup call to entrepreneurship in Nigeria is overwhelming. Entrepreneurship has been described as the ability of a nation's citizens and of foreign investors to engage in building new businesses or in restructuring existing establishments in order to adjust to changes in the economic and political environment. This is the latest trend among growing economies, and fore runner countries like Rwanda are evidence that the path of entrepreneurship is reshaping the world.

In Nigeria, shaping the future beyond oil is critical as this would enable the country to explore other opportunities for diversification of the economy. With the issue of high unemployment rates in Nigeria, drastic measures are needed to alleviate the toll unemployment has had on the economy and the society as a whole. Poverty, crime, disease, and every other societal evil can be traced directly or indirectly to unemployment. As it is aptly stated, "an idle mind is the devil's workshop."

Nigeria has a labor force of 47 million people and as this number grows, so does the rate of unemployment which is currently at about 20%. Bearing this in mind, the country is faced with the stark need to constantly create new jobs and to diversify industrial and commercial sectors to take advantage of the human and natural resources available to meet the pressing demands of tons of young men and women flung into the labor market each year. Curiously, Nigeria is better placed to develop a well-diversified economy than possibly any other country in West Africa. The abundance of natural resources, mineral deposits and fertile land it enjoys is unrivalled, as is its substantial human resource pool.

A range of initiatives devoted to promoting other sectors of the economy is already in place as part of the government's extensive reforms programme. The non-oil economy saw two-fold growth to 7% between 2001 and 2006, an encouraging sign in view of Nigeria's Vision 2020 goal of accelerated growth and economic consolidation. Optimising resource and raw material utilisation by developing a mass base of interlinked enterprises is central to this scheme. The dream of creating a world-class economy is achievable for Nigerians given the right policy atmosphere. It is recommended that all students in Nigeria should study entrepreneurship as part of their curriculum regardless of their major subject. Nigeria has historically depended on oil revenues which hardly trickle down to the common man in the village or the street. It was not until recently that the country diversified from oil dependence and is steering toward a more business based economy. According to Nigeria's Ministry of Education, the past few years have witnessed 60% of university graduates losing out on employment opportunities. This has turned out to be a boon for the economy because a large number of these graduates are establishing entrepreneurial ventures. Agricultural expansion is critical to economic prosperity across Africa, considering the region's crippling poverty levels.

A 2003 conference organised by New Partnership for Africa's Development (NEPAD) in South Africa strongly urged the promotion of cassava cultivation as a poverty eradication tool across the continent. The recommendation is based on a strategy that focuses on markets, private sector participation and research to drive a pan-African cassava initiative. What was once a rural staple and famine-reserve food has become a lucrative cash crop!

The NEPAD initiative has strong relevance for Nigeria, the world's largest cassava producer. With its large rural population and extensive farmlands, the country boasts unrivalled opportunities of transforming the humble cassava into an industrial raw material for both domestic and international markets. There is a growing and well-justified belief that the crop can transform rural economies, spur rapid economic and industrial growth and assist disadvantaged communities. While production grew steadily between 1980 and 2002 from 10,000 MT to over 35,000 MT, there is room for significant increase by bringing more land under cassava cultivation. Nigeria must take the lead not only in developing better production, harvesting and processing technologies, but also in finding new uses and markets for what is undoubtedly a wonder crop. Nigeria will make giant strides towards inclusive and sustainable development simply through the intelligent and judicious promotion of cassava farming. Nigeria's agricultural potential is enormous partly because over 90% of its 91 million hectares of total land area is arable. While soil fertility is generally estimated on the lower side, the UN Food and Agriculture Organisation (FAO) predicts medium to high yields across the country with optimal utilisation of resources. Combined with Nigeria's substantial rural population traditionally involved in agriculture, this projection translates to gigantic prospects in terms of agricultural productivity and, by extension, economic resurgence.

The fundamental problem with the Nigerian economy is its failure to diversify. Instead of investing oil revenues in multi-sector economic growth or poverty alleviation, past governments frittered away national profits through unsustainable import reliance and corruption. The resulting fragility has been clearly evident over the last year as the global economic downturn severely impacted every aspect of the Nigerian economy – from banking and foreign exchange reserves to the capital market and the mortgage sector. Reforms introduced since 1999 have produced encouraging results – most prominently, the revival of agriculture which now contributes 42% of GDP. However, and although an estimated two-thirds of the population are dependent on it for primary livelihood, Nigerian agriculture, like many other potentially high-growth sectors, continues to be a labour-intensive and low productivity operation. If embraced, the entrepreneurial revolution will not only alleviate poverty but expedite growth and diversity. In order for Nigeria as well as the whole of Africa to use trade as a platform for development and poverty eradication, some goals need to be put in place. The following are some policies that can enhance entrepreneurship:

- Lowering the overall cost of doing business by reducing bureaucratic red tape. In most African countries, there are many bureaucratic practices that stifle the process of setting up and maintaining a business. This red tape discourages entrepreneurs from investing. To combat this, some countries have already established a single business license.

- Improvement of infrastructure is necessary in creating an environment that favours business practices. Factors such as power, road network, security and others can influence whether trade can thrive or not. Without proper infrastructure, both foreign and local investment is greatly hampered.

- Varied sources of venture capital to finance business start-ups and to assist in expanding already existing businesses must abound. In addition, mentorship organisations should be established all over and not only in the metropolitan areas. The political will has to exist to ensure that policies and legislations related to trade are pushed to the forefront to ensure that they are implemented. The political class needs to take leadership in this effort because they are the ones with the authority to make the right decisions.

- Hence when the need for government and society to work together to build an entrepreneurial partnership is satisfied, we would create an environment that is more empowered and productive for women to do business.

Chapter Six

EMPOWER YOURSELF, JOIN THE E.R

"All life is a chance. So take it! The person who goes furthest is the one who is willing to do and dare."

Dale Carnegie

As stated in the quote above, *"all life is a chance, so take it."* The journey into enterprise is a chance – a chance to direct one's destiny, to chart a new course, to present one's values, and to bravely confront the world on our own terms. As individuals, we must forget our fears of the risks associated with entrepreneurship. We must recognise that the biggest risk we take with our lives is the fear of taking a risk on ourselves, our future, and our talents. As individuals, we must get beyond our mindset of dependency. We will not get out of poverty by relying on handouts from charities or expecting the government to provide for us. World Bank President Robert Zoellick says the world economy cannot meet its full growth potential, if it fails to advance the prospects of women. He said empowering women is not only the right thing to do, but it's also *"smart economics"*. As true as this statement is, women should make attempts at embracing their own financial futures and striving to work it out despite challenges. As individuals, men and women alike, we must be self-motivated and self-actualised. We must turn our individual passions and visions into productive enterprises. We must get beyond our consumer mentality and develop the mindset of an entrepreneur, a creator of goods and services.

In this chapter we will attempt to define key terms and also discuss various business options that are open to any woman who decides to launch into the world of entrepreneurship. Although there are countless numbers of definitions for an entrepreneur, as a practicing one, I believe an entrepreneur is someone who uses their inventiveness or resourcefulness if you will, to create economic value for the benefit of themselves and the society. Some other schools of thought believe that an Entrepreneur is someone who:

- **Assumes** the financial risk of the initiation, operation and management of a business(Entrepreneur.com)

- **Launches** enterprises that commercialise new products, services, or processes that contribute to economic growth. (Baumol)

- **Perceives** the market opportunity and then has the motivation, drive and ability to mobilise resources to meet it.(DiMasi)

- **Undertakes** a wealth creating and value adding process, through incubating ideas, assembling resources and making things happen.(Tan, quoting Kao)

Going by these definitions we can therefore state that an entrepreneur is a person who is driven to establish a business to take advantage of the financial opportunities and personal fulfillment offered, by pursuing their own dreams and shaping their own destiny in local, national and global economies.

Entrepreneurship

Entrepreneurship is a somewhat vague concept. At core, it involves both the actions and outlook of entrepreneurs. Beginning from the earliest known definition in the eighteenth century, entrepreneurship is said to involve risk taking, bringing together the factors of production, business innovation, and enterprise start up (Di-Masi). According to Kotelnikov, Entrepreneurship is the art of finding creative profitable solutions to problems.

Entrepreneurialism

Just like Entrepreneurship, this has many definitions. It is also often used as a synonym for entrepreneurship. However, it is also seen as a cooperative relationship between government and entrepreneurs, between the public and private sectors. To successfully go about their business of enterprise startup and growth, entrepreneurs need a supportive, favorable and conducive environment to thrive. They need governments that encourage and facilitate entrepreneurship; they need an economic system that rewards the risk taker and the innovator; and they also benefit from a culture that respects and champions the entrepreneur.

In this chapter we will use entrepreneurialism to denote a capitalist, free market economy where innovation, job creation and income growth are driven by the talents and initiatives of entrepreneurs in a supportive relationship with government. These private sector individuals are supported by public policies that allow "citizens from all walks of life have the opportunity to become innovative entrepreneurs". (Baumol)

What is Entrepreneurial Revolution?

It is simply a boom in entrepreneurial thinking. A situation where everyone begins to think along the lines of business ownership and meeting needs for a profit. It is best defined as a radical and coordinated attempt to accelerate wealth creation through the promotion of innovative business practices.

Describing it further, E.R is also a point of convergence when and where a great number of entrepreneurs will put into motion an irreversible chain reaction of productive ventures outside the limits of cynicism and fear. The objective of this revolution is rapid and sustainable economic expansion with a special focus on unique and creatively evolved business models. It is this entrepreneurial spirit that is empowering countries like China, India alongside Russia and the Former Soviet Satellite Countries in Eastern Europe and the Baltic States to rise above the gravity of years of under employment, and centralised control of the economy.

Can anyone become an entrepreneur?

The answer to that is yes but first, we will examine what it takes to be an entrepreneur and whether or not, you, the reader have an entrepreneurial spirit. Before you despair, the good news is that you can learn to be entrepreneurial but you need to assess where you are so that you know what you need to learn. An entrepreneur is a man or woman who is driven to establish a business to take advantage of the financial opportunities and personal fulfilment offered by pursuing their own dreams and shaping their own destiny in local, national and global economies.

The following is a broad list of the characteristics of an entrepreneur:

- Self-confident and multi-skilled
- Confident in the face of difficulties and discouraging circumstances
- Not an 'inventor' in the traditional sense but one who is able to carve out a new niche in the market place, often invisible to others
- Results-oriented: To be successful requires the drive that only comes from setting goals and targets and getting pleasure from achieving them
- A risk-taker: To succeed means taking measured risks
- A risk-assessor: In today's economic climate starting a business can be less risky than conventional employment
- Totally committed; a person who will do whatever it takes to be successful in business: Hard work, energy and single-mindedness are essential elements in the entrepreneurial profile
- Visionary and optimistic: In new and emerging businesses,

the person who starts the business is often an entrepreneur who believes that with the right resources you can achieve anything

- A participant, not an observer; a player, not a fan
- A course-setter: The entrepreneur likes to be in control of his/her future (Di-Masi; Entrepreneur.com)

Do you see yourself in the above listed characteristics? You can take the aptitude test in Appendix 1 to give you a clearer understanding of where you stand as an entrepreneur. Given that you have evaluated your entrepreneurial strengths and weaknesses, let's begin to lay the building blocks for your entrepreneurial journey.

Practical steps to starting a business

- *Ideas/Need:* To start a business you need to conceptualise what you want to venture into. There are two major ways to streamline what you want to venture into. Either through an idea you have thought out or simply through a need you have noticed in your immediate environment. There are certain situations you notice which make you most uncomfortable and which you desire strongly to correct. That could be a pointer to what you should build your new business around. For instance, a littered street or community, lack of power supply, child laborers, home deliveries for groceries etc. At the end of this book, there are over 250 business ideas that you can choose from to launch your entrepreneurial journey.

- **Write it down:** It has been proven that the faintest pen is stronger than the strongest memory. Writing your ideas and goals down commits you to a large extent to stick to achieving them. Writing down and keeping your goals where you can see them every day, is a first major step to cross on the road to accomplishing these goals. Dividing them into short, medium and long term goals will better help put these goals into perspective and further help make seemingly insurmountable targets become easier to accomplish. It is advisable and quite practicable to carry a notepad around as you go about your daily activities. This way whenever the inspiration for an idea comes into your mind, you can write it down before it slips out of your mind.

- **Get a team:** Most times, people fail in their attempt to start a business when they try to handle all the aspects of the start up by themselves without engaging help from others when necessary. The temptation to carry the burden all by one's self, in order to save money is very strong as every new entrepreneur tries to save as much as is possible. This could be a death trap for a young business especially one that involves processes. It is wise to engage the help of others when and where it is expedient that you do so.

- *Get started:* The fastest way to start your business is to just start. Breaking the initial inertia and launching out is the only way to get ahead and get going. Saying it without backing it up with actions will only leave it in the realm of wishful thinking.

- *Re-evaluate and Re-launch:* Over a period of time, preferably three months after your start up, it is advised that you take a retreat and re-assess your business. Check for pitfalls, set backs or even failures you have experienced within that period of time. If peradventure you have not experienced any of these, it is still quite necessary that you take a step back and review your performance and make adjustments where you deem fit.

How to join the Entrepreneurial Revolution

- *Develop interest in owning a business:* the very first step towards achieving any feat is having a desire or an interest. It is your interest that fuels the passion you need to get your business running and thriving. Don't jump into a business because everyone around you is doing it. This is what creates a glut in the market and a reduction in customer demand. Instead, find out what drives and motivates you. This is what will set you apart from your competition and keep you going when things get tough.

- **Get some sort of training:** having the interest is not just enough. You need to get some sort of formal training, either by studying articles, books, newsletters or watching programs that teach you how to start and run a business effectively; or via apprenticeship. Just as a tailor learns by apprenticing herself to an established tailor, find someone who has a similar business to yours and learn from them. One admonition, don't expect to learn everything you need to do in your own business from someone else; you are unique and you should let it show as you run your business in a way that is unique to you.

- **Carry out self-assessment/analysis:** what do you like to do and what would you rather someone else does for you? It is important to consider your strengths and weaknesses, temperament, personality, and other factors when starting a business. You have already responded to an assessment of your business acumen in this book; what does it tell you about your likes and dislikes? You want to start a business that compliments your personality not one that cramps your style.

- **Generate possible business ideas:** one great entrepreneur, Linus Pauling, once said that, *"the best way to have a good idea is to have lots of ideas."* Brainstorm with family or friends what ideas are out there for a good business. This would generate many results, most of which you will discard. Pick the one that aligns most with your passion and personality. If you are one of those chronic procrastinators and you have ideas but have not taken any concrete steps to start your own business, it is time to do so.

On the other hand, if your family and friends do not provide ideas that resonate with your passion, you may be wondering where to find better ideas.

Here are some tips:

1. Write out what is on your mind. Whether you will ultimately discard these initial ideas is not the problem; discover them first before you criticise The more ideas you start with, the better.

2. If your mind is blank or you do not have the faintest idea of what business to go into, then you should try asking yourself some questions such as:

- What education have you received?
- What inspires you?
- What skills do you possess?
- What are your talents?
- What do people praise you for doing?
- What past or present career positions provide you with work experience you can use?

- What jobs and chores do you like to do?

Your ability to answer these questions will reveal to you, your personal business assets. Then write down a list of some goods and services that can be created and sold from them. Also you may not generate an idea, but you may see a need and work towards filling it; that is, take advantage of opportunities. In generating ideas, remember that *anything you can do well could be turned into a business.*

Once you have decided on your business idea, plan how you will bring your idea to life – write a business plan. There is a popular saying that *"he who fails to plan, plans to fail"* This is true even in business. No responsible person undertakes any venture without proper planning. After you have zeroed in on your hot business idea, a business plan allows you to look at the feasibility of your idea, and then assess possible risks that may arise and work out strategies on how to tackle them.

Planning improves the probability of success. *A business plan is a written document that clearly defines the goals of a business and outlines the methods for achieving them.* The business plan is like a compass guiding you through your business journey.

A business plan is important for these reasons:

- It is a concrete step when starting your business
- Helps to clarify your thinking
- Enhances your commitment
- Helps you chart a steady course in line with your objectives
- Acts as a management and financial blueprint
- Helps avoid costly mistakes

Essentially, a business plan must comprise of the following sections:

1. **Executive Summary:** a two-page summary of your business and its activities.

2. **Business Description:** an overview of your business. How will your business grow and profit?

3. **Market and Competition:** this is the largest section and should detail competition and how you will do better than them.

4. **Product or Service:** describe the core of your business. What product or service will you be providing in the market-place?

5. **Marketing/Selling:** explains how you will reach your customers. Will you advertise, establish a website, or network? You

should plan to do all three and more.

6. Management and Personnel: details your staff qualifications. What qualifies you to run this business?

7. Financial Data: contains your balance sheet, profit-and-loss statement, and other financial information about your business.

8. Appendices: attach other documents that will be relevant to your type of business. For further details on how to write a business plan, you may wish to refer to my book, How to Write a Business Plan.

Once you have completed your business plan, you will have a fair idea of how much it would cost you to start your business. You would need to consider how to get the money, either through loans, from family, banks, or from your personal savings. Here are some ways to raise money for your business venture:

Six Tactics for Starting a Business with No/Minimal Capital

1. Learn to make sacrifices

The reality is that starting a business entails a lot of sacrifice and cutting back on your lifestyle. Once you have set a deadline to launch your business, you have to learn to live on less and put money aside to fund the business.

2. Back Yourself

An entrepreneur who is not willing to invest her own money into her business does not believe in herself and would not inspire anyone else to invest in her business. Once you can invest your personal resources into your business, you can expect support from close relatives and friends who believe in you and know the amount of money you have pumped into the business, which is a clear indication of your commitment to make the business succeed.

3. DIY (Do-It-Yourself)

An entrepreneur at the start-up stage must endeavour to be jack-of-all-trades. Even if you have your own specialty, do everything it takes to make your business succeed. The more you do, the less you need to pay someone else to do for you. This can help you save some money and get the business off the ground. The entrepreneur and the management team at the start-up stage must train themselves to do most of the work instead of outsourcing.

4. Work in Parallel

At the start-up stage of your business, you can sell your time to raise some money while you are building your business from the income generated from the consulting work.

5. Keep the End in Mind

Although consulting can generate some money for a start-up business, there is a possibility of being over dependence and forgetting the big picture of developing your own brand. This means the entrepreneur becomes greedy and caught up in a cycle of selling more time with fewer opportunities, to sell the business for long-term.

6. Focus on cash flow, not profitability

It is a generally accepted norm that, profit is the key to survival of a business but in reality business relies on cash for the day-to-day running of the establishment. Therefore focus on cash flow. Cash is the king, queen and prince of every business. Let us now review pitfalls or mistakes you should avoid when starting your business.

Pitfalls To Avoid When Starting Your Business

Though your business is unique to you, it is not so unique that you cannot find similarities with other businesses. For starters, the basic objective of any business enterprise is to make money. Thus, it is how you plan to make money that differs. The following are some errors you should strive to avoid, that people in business make:

- **Not listening to those who know the ropes**

It is important to believe in yourself when starting your business, but don't become too self-assured. One of the most humbling realisations is that you do not have all the answers! Seek out professionals such as lawyers that can help you deal with some of the technical aspects of your business. It is also wise to seek out individuals directly involved in your industry who can provide insights into the operation of your business and the demographics of your clientele.

- **Lacking a business plan**

As we stated earlier, your business plan will provide you with a blueprint for your idea. Sure, you can run a business without ever writing out a plan, however, a plan helps you to see the big picture, plan for contingencies and obtain funding. Your business will be better off with a plan. On the other hand, don't get so caught up in writing a business plan that you never get round to putting the plan into action.

- **Lacking funding**

Inadequate planning may lead to lack of funding for start up or expansion. It may also lead to a lack of adequate financial savings to cushion inevitable rough spots in a business cycle. Situating your business in a bad spot. All business owners should find a location that is both easily accessible and highly visible to potential clientele. When picking out your site, keep in mind the changing needs of you and your customers, the possible addition of competitors to your area, and the image surrounding the businesses project. Also consider the duration of each lease you are asked to begin or renew.

- **Not knowing who your customers are**

Before you begin advertising, consider the audience that you are trying to reach. Understand who they are and what it is about your product or service that will interest them. From there, create a marketing angle that will cater directly to your target audience. Starting this early and continuously adjusting your marketing plan based on what you learn in the marketplace is ideal.

- **Not maintaining your brand while marketing**

When establishing yourself in the public's eye, be sure to maintain the same marketing image throughout every form of advertising. Marketing solely on TV, in print, or on the Internet will limit your potential audience. Show your "face" by combining several forms of media to reach a broader spectrum of clientele. And time new marketing campaigns with the release of new products and services, discounts, seasonal sales and upcoming events that will help you to generate business.

- **Confusing marketing campaigns**

Remember the phrase "keep it simple"? This idea applies to marketing. The catchiest slogan or most imaginative ad is futile if no one gets it. And remember: if it sounds too good to be true, it probably is. Do not oversell your product or make promises you cannot keep; the public is more informed today than they've ever been.

- **Not knowing who to market to**

People go into business because they believe they have something unique to offer to the world. Do not assume that everyone will share your level of passion about your product or service! By knowing and understanding your target audience you can gear your advertising toward them. Attempting to win absolutely everyone over to your product or service is not a reasonable goal. Any new marketing technique should be tested first—perhaps by utilising a focus group—and then adjusted according to the feedback you receive.

- **Forgetting your established client base**

Did you know that 80 percent of customers are repeat business? Don't make the mistake of focusing solely on new prospects and neglecting your existing clientele. They are the reason you've made it this far! Occasionally rewarding them for their loyalty to your business with perks new customers don't receive is a nice way to say 'thank you'.

- **Ineffective marketing feedback**

It's difficult to know whether your marketing strategies are working if you're not doing the proper follow-up. Often failure to follow up, leads to businesses changing strategies unnecessarily, thinking a change will result in a better turnout. However, the tried-and-true formula typically works best and you shouldn't give up on it! Establishing your brand means building a reputation that your target audience will begin to expect and rely on.

- **Not keeping a close eye on finances**

The waiting period between the onset of a business and the influx of revenue doesn't escape any new business. It's imperative that during this time you make sure you have a financial cushion for personal expenses as well as enough funds for the start-up costs. Avoid just charging the credit cards, as doing so will only incur interest on top of your expenses, as well as bad debt if you don't have the money to settle the account. Making rash spending decisions (like throwing your entire budget to that amazing Super Bowl ad) will hurt more than help if you have no money left for daily costs of operation or emergencies.

- **Not addressing outstanding customer balances**

Knowing how to aggressively and successfully collect on delinquent accounts without damaging customer relationships is absolutely essential. If you're too afraid to talk money or to risk offending a non-payer, your business will fail. If you haven't received payment at least 30 days from issuing the invoice, issue another. It's always possible they didn't get the first, or simply filed it away and forgot the debt entirely. Remember: it's not personal; it's just business.

- **Not knowing how to say "no"**

No one can perform all the necessary daily tasks when running a business. People will constantly request things of you, and you will simply have to learn how to say "no." Your productivity will decline if you are stopping every five minutes to do something for someone else. There are self-assertiveness classes you can sign up for if you feel you need a little help in this area.

- **Doing all the work**

See which of your tasks you can delegate to others that would better suit someone else's talents. Doling out those secretarial duties and mindless tasks will result in streamlining your day and your profitability. There's no need to stress yourself out by attempting to do everything on your own. Hire a receptionist, accountant, or store clerk. Use your employees wisely and keep the important things only you can do on your plate.

- **Conducting empty meetings**

Too many businesses conduct meetings that pull everyone away from their duties to discuss unimportant issues, all in the name of productivity. Make sure your meetings have an agenda, a clearly defined outcome, occur only when necessary and involve only those people that need to be there. Everyone will be more in tune, and your business will run more smoothly.

- **Fear**

Perhaps the single most destructive force to any business venture is fear. If you are afraid to take risks, you will never succeed in your business. You must let go of excuses, procrastination and doubt in order to achieve business success. Don't make a habit of postponing what you know needs to be done just because you are afraid to take a bold step. As the saying goes; *nothing ventured, nothing gained.*

Chapter Seven

BALANCING IT ALL: A HOME BUSINESS MODEL

"There is only one success – to be able to spend your life in your own way."

Christopher Morley

As mentioned earlier, women's family responsibilities often clash with their entrepreneurial goals. Thus, it is highly necessary to balance both of these sides of women's lives – business aspirations and family responsibilities. According to a school of thought, women have been designed to be home makers and men, home builders. The saying that ''the place of the woman is in the home' has drawn a lot of opposition and outcry from women all over the world who believe that women can and should be given the chance to explore their chances in their chosen paths and careers.

We will be putting into consideration, the fact that women are home builders and should, as much as possible, be around their homes more for the sake of their children and their family as a whole. This may not be a very popular view but we strongly believe that the presence of an adult especially the mother in a home goes a long way in determining the outcome of the lives of children and younger members of the family.

Because women are instrumental to the growth and development of human beings who in turn make up society, there has been a tussle over whether they do belong solely to the confines of the home; bringing up children and moulding characters or to the corporate world taking up roles and handling responsibilities. Recent events all around the world have shown the impact of the absent parents in the lives of young men and women - violence, loss of character and misplaced values, thuggery, and increased crime rates.

On the other hand, though we all understand the need for someone to take care of children, women are afraid of being abandoned after they make the decision to stay home. A survey carried out among young contemporary women shows that the majority of them prefer to be out in the corporate world fending for themselves rather than having to depend solely on their husbands or the men in their lives for sustenance.

In order to balance the need to work and to stay home, we introduce an economically viable option - Cottage industry. A woman can put her skills and expertise to use from home earning a fair income and at the same time keeping close tabs on the welfare of her home. It is possible to be economically relevant and still be a content woman fulfilling her traditional role of raising a healthy family - healthy in both mind and body. This must begin first with an acceptance of the fact that the responsibility of home making is respectable, vital to human and societal development and not a punishment at all. It is a duty much associated with the woman. It is not degrading at all neither is it something to be ashamed of.

BENEFITS OF WORKING FROM HOME

There are many attendant benefits that come with working from home. Let me start by clarifying this concept of working from home. This kind of business is referred to as Cottage Industry - an industry where the creation of products and services is home-based, rather than factory-based.

There are a plethora of things that women and even men can do to earn an income from the comfort of their homes. These can be fashioned into fully functional firms or manufacturing outfits. These categories of businesses are known as 'Cottage Industries'. These have been described as being the major source of economic growth in countries like China. Working from home affords individuals a lot of opportunities like the ones listed below:

Personal Freedom

This is a very enticing benefit that mostly drives individuals into venturing into running home based businesses. The ability to gain control over one's life is perhaps the most attractive aspect of working from home. Rather than bending to the demands of the work environment, individuals can mould their environments to meet their own needs. Instead of adapting to a nine-to-five iron clad time structure, a home based worker can construct his or her time schedule to fit personal needs and comfort.

Time, which is often referred to as 'not our friend' suddenly becomes a lot easier to manipulate. The pressure to finish up what you're doing before closing time, or to look busy even when you're not, is eliminated. As a home-based businessperson, you determine your own hours. As a home-based worker, you have greater control over not only your time but also your environment.

Strengthening Family Ties

In many instances, home-based businesses are strengthening family relationships by enabling the whole family to get involved. Instead of going in separate directions, more and more husbands and wives are pooling their energies and working toward a common goal. At the same time, children have an opportunity to see what their parents do for a living and to learn about business firsthand.

Increase in Productivity

Home-based businesspersons are more productive. They have a higher output level. Part of the reason for this is that there's simply more time available. Hours that would normally be spent commuting to and from the office can be used to run the business instead. Another reason that can't be overlooked is the increased level of enthusiasm on the part of home-based workers. Many get so caught up in what they're doing that it's actually hard for them to stop. This deep commitment is scarcely found when working for someone else.

Job Security

With corporate downsizing and mergers going on all over the world threatening job security, many workers have come to realise that the best job security of all is a business of their own. Rather than worrying whether their industries will be hit next or trying to find other jobs after being laid off, they are creating their own work as home-based entrepreneurs.

More Freedom

This is definitely one of the best advantages of having a home-based business. You can take a vacation whenever you want and work whenever you want. As long as you are producing, it does not matter when or how you work. Your time is really YOUR time; that is something you can never have as an employee.

Reduced Stress

Choosing to work from home can go a long way in drastically reducing stress and its consequences. Especially, stress that stems from having to juggle various responsibilities like being a mother, wife and a professional or executive, at one job or another, all at once.

Competitive Advantage

Working out of your home can enable you to be more competitive, not just in the prices you charge but also in the quality of service you offer. You can use the money you save on rent to increase your overall profitability, or you can pass it on to customers in the form of lower prices. Competitors restricted by higher overhead costs have no such options. What they charge is predetermined by their rental agreements.

Financial Benefits

The financial benefits of working at home are very attractive. Instead of waiting for an employer to give you a raise or a promotion, the amount of money you can earn is directly related to your own performance.

Irrespective of whether the home based business is your major source of income or simply an extra source, working from your home ensures that you are solely responsible for the level of output your business experiences. What's more, individuals who have had no headway with the labour market can set up their own business and earn an income from it e.g.—homemakers, students, retirees, and the disabled.

In addition to the money you can earn, by working at home, you also save on money that would have been spent on work accessories such as transportation, clothes, eating out, etc. These costs could run into several hundreds even thousands within time. Having your business in your home also makes it easier to provide customers with personal service or provide necessary information. When customers come to see you, they can be welcomed into an atmosphere that is warm and inviting. Given these benefits and more, the trend toward home-based businesses is clearly just beginning. Those who have recognised the opportunities existing under their own roofs are in the forefront of a growing movement The dream of owning your own business, a dream thought by many to be unattainable, is not only within your sight but at your doorstep. You really do not need to look any further than your kitchen, bedroom, den, living room or garage to find the foundation on which to build your business enterprise.

CHALLENGES TO WORKING FROM HOME

Well, it is quite important to add at this point that working from is not an entire walk over, as there are some down sides to it too. The most important thing here is to recognise them and work at eliminating or controlling them as much as possible.

1. You Handle All the Work Alone

In a conventional company with an organisational structure different tasks are delegated to employees. In a home-based-business, the entrepreneur handles all of these tasks on his or her own. This workload is elevated to an even higher degree if your business gains momentum and grows. All the mundane and repetitive tasks from the administrative to the operational activities are handled solely by you, the home-based-business owner.

2. Home Life and Work Life Merge

If your business is based in an office sometime in the evening you can close the door, go home and leave the work in the office until the next morning. But working from home poses a different scenario altogether. Your home life unwittingly becomes your work life. No matter where you are in your home, the attraction of checking if you made any sales, or sending an email, or discussing projects with your freelancers becomes strong; and it also becomes difficult to restrain this urge.

3. Constant Distractions

In the home environment there are quite a number of things that could hinder your concentration, dogs barking, kids playing, and loud music from your neighbour or from the record store close to your home or a wide variety of other distractions. These distractions can hamper your ability to concentrate on the job at hand.

It is clearly evident that starting a business from home presents numerous challenges, but if the venture is approached correctly, it could lead to the beginning of a prosperous and prominent establishment.

Chapter Eight

WOMEN WHO MADE IT

"The big secret in life is that there is no big secret. Whatever your goal, you can get there if you're willing to work."

Oprah Winfrey

There are several examples of women in history and in present time who have blazed the trail in their pursuit for entrepreneurial and leadership endeavours Some of them built their enterprises from the comfort of their homes while others went out into the public sphere. Neither time nor space will permit a listing of each and every one of these amazons but here are a few examples from around the world:

Oprah Winfrey

Born poor and black in Mississippi in 1954, she learned to read and write from home. At 17, she began working as a reporter for a local radio station. She was a bright and entrepreneurial kid. At 18, she won the Miss Black Tennessee beauty pageant. At 19, she was anchoring a newscast on Nashville's WTVF-TV. She later co-anchored the nightly newscast at WJZ-TV in Baltimore, and co-hosted a local talk show called People Are Talking, before jumping to Chicago's WLS-TV.

Her morning talk show in Chicago debuted in 1984 and rose to number one in the ratings within a month. Winfrey's talk show, Oprah went national in 1986 and took top spot almost immediately. After reigning as the queen of daytime talk for 25 seasons, Winfrey went on to start her own television station, Oprah Winfrey Network (OWN). She is very charitable, supporting many worthy causes including funding a girl's school in South Africa.

10 Things Small Business Owners Can Learn From Oprah

Oprah Winfrey, who has being described as the wealthiest black woman, has over the years shown great business skills and acumen worthy of emulation. The following are some vital things we can learn from her as a business person and as a woman. "Forget about the fast lane. If you really want to fly, harness your power to your passion. Honour your calling. Everybody has one. Trust your heart, and success will come to you." Oprah According to her, everybody has a calling. And your real job in life is to figure out what this is and get about the business of doing it.

The thing is, once you are truly connected to your purpose in life, the business becomes easy. It's easy to make choices, it's easy to know what to do next (though not always so easy to work up the courage to do it!) and it's easy to keep your energy focused on your business. Are you following your true calling?

"Let your light shine. Shine within you so that it can shine on someone else. Let your light shine"
- Oprah

2. Inspiration sells

Oprah had a genius for keeping her show all about the positive. She never got stuck in the mire like other talk show hosts and dedicated her life to using her platform to inspire and educate others. Some believe that people don't buy feeling good. Oprah proves this wrong, and shows us that feeling good can sell too! Does your marketing and content make people feel good about themselves?

"If it doesn't feel right, don't do it. That's the lesson. That lesson alone will save you a lot of grief. Even doubt means don't."
- Oprah

3. Be true to yourself

Oprah was constantly barraged with opportunities that did not meet with her focus and objectives for the show. She was approached by numerous people wanting to get on her show. But she was very clear on what did and did not constitute an Oprah show and only did the shows that reflected her values and her brand. By staying true to herself and her show's values, she was able to keep the quality of the show high. Are you making compromises in your business that do not feel right? If you have deviated from your initial vision for your business, the best time to retrace your steps is now.

"Surround yourself with only people who are going to lift you higher." - Oprah

4. Use multiple channels

While we may not all have Oprah's budget and reach, we can use the channels that are available to us to spread our good word and work. Oprah used TV, Radio, her website, YouTube, Twitter and her magazine O very powerfully to spread her message. The great thing about this is that if one way wasn't available or didn't fit with her target market, there were a multitude of others that would. What other channels could you be using to market your business?

"Follow your instincts. That's where true wisdom manifests itself."
- Oprah

5. Act quickly when something isn't working

Oprah was warm and engaging on stage, but make no mistake, she was an incredibly savvy business woman and she was quick to make a change when something wasn't working in one of her businesses. Earlier this year, Oprah launched OWN, The Oprah Winfrey Network, a television in partnership with Discovery Networks. When network ratings were slow, the Network head Christina Norman left rather abruptly after only 4 months in the job. Do you make hard decisions quickly in your business?

"When someone shows you who they are, believe them the first time." - Oprah

6. Put YOU into your business

The reason that Oprah had such a long and successful show on TV was because she was real and easy to relate to. She was true to herself in everything that she did and made herself very approachable through her warmth and connection with her audience. Everyone who watched her show felt like they knew her, like she was their friend. And in many respects she was. How can you put more of yourself into your business? How can you make your clients and colleagues feel like they know the real you? Can they think of you as a friend?

"The big secret in life is that there is no big secret. Whatever your goal, you can get there if you're willing to work." - Oprah

7. Work hard

There is no doubt that Oprah worked hard. In 25 years of taping, she never missed a show, not once! Every day, she would show up at 6:00am, no matter what. It is reported that her executive assistant clocked up over 800 hours of overtime between January and April one year, that's a 12.5 hour work day! If her assistant was putting in this kind of time, you can bet Oprah was putting in more. In the preparation video that Oprah shares on her site, she shares how grateful she is to be able to go out and buy herself a coffee before her meeting that day, and how she is looking forward to spending some time with her friends. In 25 years, Oprah was consumed by her work and it is clear that she would not have achieved the level of success that she did without that dedication to her craft. Could you be putting more into your business? Are there opportunities for extra commitment on your part?

"Do the one thing you think you cannot do. Fail at it. Try again. Do better the second time. The only people who never tumble are those who never mount the high wire. This is your moment. Own it." - Oprah

8. Keep on keeping on

This is the other side of acting quickly when something isn't working. Oprah never sat back and left her fate to the gods. She lived through an atrocious childhood, faced racism and sexism early in her career and yet still she prevailed. She never gave up on dreams. Success does not happen overnight (much as we might wish it did!), it takes time, effort and showing up. It was these challenges that made Oprah the woman that she is today. These challenges gave her the strength of character, self-determination and resilience that she is known for. Are there areas in your business that could use more focus and persistence?

"Devote today to something so daring even you can't believe you're doing it." - Oprah

9. Be Bold

Oprah committed to everything she did 100%, whether she knew it was going to work or not. One of her great philosophies is that we miss out on life if we don't take risks and she is doing exactly this by leaving her show to focus on her new OWN network. Make no mistake; even for someone of Oprah's stature this is an enormous risk, but exciting for her as well. I am sure that she is looking forward to the challenge that this new venture is giving her.

"I've come to believe that each of us has a personal calling that's as unique as a fingerprint – and that the best way to succeed is to discover what you love and then find a way to offer it to others in the form of service, working hard, and also allowing the energy of the universe to lead you." - Oprah

10. Leave them wanting more

Oprah retired from her show at the top of her game. She easily could have continued for years, very successfully, but instead she decided to leave while her show is still the number 1 daytime talk show in the USA. Oprah knew her time had come and decided to step down while she was still at the top. This allows her to now focus on her other ventures and move onto the next stage in her life. By making herself less available on regular TV, I'm sure she will use her new channel to maintain her presence in people's lives. How best can you use your business to touch the lives of people around you and make an impact in your environment?

PRINCESS STELLA ODUAH

Considered an Amazon of a woman, Princess Oduah has conquered the private sector in Nigeria and successfully established the conglomerate; Sea Petroleum and Gas Group of Companies, as an enviable group of companies with interest spanning Oil and Gas, Agriculture, Engineering, Logistics and Trading. During her years in private enterprise, Princess Stella was a major employer of labour with her businesses touching lives every day. She is today the sole sponsor of the Joe Life Foundation; a cluster of charitable efforts that are today affecting lives across Nigeria. Currently, Princess Stella is bringing her wealth of knowledge and real world experience to help manage Nigeria's all-too-important Aviation Industry as Honourable Minister of the Federal Ministry of Aviation.

NGOZI OKONJO IWEALA

Born into a royal family from Delta State of Nigeria, Ngozi Okonjo Iweala spent her early years living with her grandparents while her parents studied abroad. At the completion of their studies, the family moved to Ibadan where her parents took up jobs at the then University College of Ibadan now University of Ibadan.

Though the civil war disrupted her education it did not slow her down, she passed her A levels with good grades and was admitted into Harvard University to study Economics. Leaving the shores of the country, Ngozi Okonjo Iweala performed exceptionally well in school and Graduated with good grades. She has a Ph.D. from the Michigan Institute of Technology.

Her first experience in the World Bank came through an internship program. She continued there with a 21-year career as a development economist at the World Bank, where she held the posts of Vice President and Corporate Secretary.

Following her role as Vice President in the World Bank, the then Nigerian President Olusegun Obasanjo requested her to serve as Nigerian Minister of Finance. She held this position between 2003 and 2006. In this period, she introduced economic reforms policy in Nigeria. She initiated the practice of publishing allocations from to the federal government to each state in the country. Okonjo-Iweala was instrumental in boosting Nigeria's credit rating on Fitch and Standard and Poor's rankings to BB minus. She headed a team that renegotiated the cancellation of about 60 percent of Nigeria's external debt with the Paris Club to the tune of US $18 billion.

After her resignation as Minister of Finance she founded NOI Consulting and also co-founded Makeda Funds with SEAF. The Fund was designed to help and support small businesses in emerging markets. She left NOI consulting to serve as Managing Director of the World Bank. She is married to a surgeon and together they have four children, three boys and a girl. Ngozi Okonjo-Iweala is a professional who is worth her salt, she doubles also as a true African as she mostly favours African print fabrics than any other kind.

ANGELA MERKEL

Angela Merkel, the first German female to attain the position, is the present Chancellor of Germany. She is also credited with being the youngest person to be German chancellor since the Second World War. Angela was elected to the German Parliament from Mecklenburg-Vorpommern and since April 2000, has also been holding the title of the Chairwoman of the Christian Democratic Union (CDU).

Angela Merkel studied physics in Templin and at the University of Leipzig, from 1973 to 1978. For the next two years, from 1978 to 1990, she worked and studied at the Central Institute for Physical Chemistry of the Academy of Sciences, in Berlin-Adlershof. In 1977, she married the physics student Ulrich Merkel, but got divorced in 1982. Angela has done doctoral thesis on Quantum Chemistry and received a doctorate for the same and also undertaken research work. She married Joachim Sauer, a chemistry professor in 1988.

Angela Merkel stepped into politics in 1989, when she joined the new party Demokratischer Aufbruch, after the fall of the Berlin Wall. After the first (and the only) democratic election of the East German state, she became the deputy spokesperson of the new pre-unification caretaker government, under Lothar de Maizière.

She became Minister for Women and Youth in Helmut Kohl's 3rd cabinet, after her party's merger with West German CDU. In 1994, she was made Minister for the Environment and Reactor Safety, the post which served as a foundation of her political career. With the defeat of the Kohl government, in the 1998 general election, Merkel was made the Secretary-General of the CDU. A financial scandal rocked her party in 1999, after which she advocated a fresh start without her mentor, Kohl, and was elected to become the first female chairperson of the party.

Angela Merkel was sworn in as the 'Chancellor of Germany' on 22nd November 2005. She leads a grand coalition, comprising of CDU's sister party, the Christian Social Union (CSU) and the Social Democratic Party of Germany (SPD). She has been following pro-free-market reform agenda since then, apart from advocating a strong German-American relationship. She has made serious efforts to overhaul the government's health care system, along with the burdensome corporate tax policies. Merkel has also made her strict budgetary impact on the extensive European Union budget debates. In 2007, she offered Europe's help to get Israel and the Palestinians back to the negotiating table. Recently, she expressed Germany's support for Israel, during a speech to the Knesset.

Angela Merkel was named as the 'Most Powerful Woman of the World' in 2007, by Forbes Magazine, for the second consecutive time. She is the third woman to serve on the G8, after Margaret Thatcher and Kim Campbell. In 2007, Angela became the second woman to chair a G8 summit, after Margaret Thatcher. She has served as the president of the European Council and in 2007, became a member of the 'Council of Women World Leaders'.

CONDOLEEZZA RICE

Secretary of State from 2005 until 2009 under President George W. Bush, Condoleezza Rice was born in Birmingham, Alabama on 14 November 1954. She was the first African-American woman to hold the position of Secretary of State. As a child, Rice was a gifted student and a prodigy on the piano, and she entered college at the age of 15 with the intention of becoming a concert pianist. Along the way, she was influenced by political scientist Josef Korbel, the father of former U.S. Secretary of State Madeleine Albright. Rice changed her plans and studied international politics, and by the early 1980s she was teaching at Stanford University and becoming a prominent public voice on international affairs. She also worked with the Pentagon and with the administration of George Bush, the elder, as an expert on foreign affairs. She returned to Stanford during the Bill Clinton administration before being tapped as National Security Advisor by the younger President Bush. In January of 2005, after Bush was elected to a second term, Rice replaced Colin Powell as Secretary of State and served until the end of Bush's term. She then joined the lecture circuit and took a position as a professor at the Hoover Institution in Stanford University.

Rice had an oil tanker named after her while she was a member of the Chevron Corporation board of directors during the 1990s. She remains a talented musician; in 2002 she performed a concert in Washington, D.C. with cellist Yo Yo Ma.

ELLEN JOHNSON SIRLEAF

The 24th President of Liberia and the first elected female Head of State in Africa, Madam Ellen Johnson Sirleaf was born in Monrovia, the capital of Liberia, an Americo-Liberian. From 1948 to 1955 Ellen Johnson studied accounts and economics at the College of West Africa in Monrovia. After marriage at the age of 17 to James Sirleaf, she travelled to America in 1961 and continued her studies, achieving a degree from the University of Colorado. From 1969 to 1971 she studied economics at Harvard, gaining a masters degree in public administration. Ellen Johnson-Sirleaf then returned to Liberia and began working in William Tolbert's (True Whig Party) government. Civil war broke out in the country in 1989 and lasted till 1996.

In 1997, she came second to Charles Taylor (gaining 10% of the vote compared to his 75%) out of a field of 14 candidates. The election was declared free and fair by international observers. By 1999, civil war had erupted to Liberia, and Taylor was accused of interfering with his neighbours, fomenting unrest and rebellion. Johnson-Sirleaf played an active role in the transitional government as the country prepared for the 2005 elections, and eventually stood for president against ex-international footballer, George Manneh Weah. On 23 November 2005, Ellen Johnson-Sirleaf was declared the winner of the Liberian election and confirmed as the country's next president. Her inauguration, attended by the likes of US First Lady Laura Bush and Secretary of

State Condoleezza Rice.

Earning a second term, Johnson-Sirleaf continues to serve as Liberia's president. She has succeeded in orchestrating the reconstruction of war-torn Liberia, reconciling warring factions, the rehabilitation of combatants and victims, and the rebuilding of social infrastructure.

HAJIYA ZAINAB MAINA

Hajiya Zainab Maina, FCIA ,MFR was born on the 7th of August 1948. She was appointed Minister of Women Affairs and Social Development of the Federal Republic of Nigeria in July 2011. She is an example of a woman who scaled the walls of gender inequality and went ahead to amass not only knowledge but also a plethora of accolades that stand her out as a woman of excellence with a strong desire for change.

Education and Personal Life

Zainab Maina hails from Adamawa state in North-East Nigeria. She was educated at foremost Nigerian polytechnic, Kaduna Polytechnic where she has Diploma in Administration and Higher National Diploma in Catering and Hotel Management. In addition, she has a certificate in Secretarial Studies from the Federal Training Centre Kaduna and also Centre for Development & Population,Washington DC,USA where she received a

Certificate in Institution Building Activities. She is married to Alhaji Umar Joji Maina, the Dan-maliki of Mubi in Adamawa State and they are blessed with children.

Prior to her ministerial appointment in July 2011,Zainab Maina served on many boards in and outside her state and in various capacities. She was Board Chairman, National Council for Nomadic Education(2009–2011); Board Chairman,Garki Microfinance Bank (1998);

Board Chairman, NCWS, Garki Microfinance Bank, Abuja(1997);

Deputy Chairman, Police Community Relations Committee FCT Command(1998-Date)

Member, Vision 2010 Committee(1997); Board Member, National Programme on Immunisation (1998–2000);

Board Member,Adamawa State Primary Schools Board(1991–1994), Board Member,Family Economic Advancement Programme(FEAP)(1997–2000).

She was the National President – National Council for Women Societies (NCWS),Nigeria(1997-2001.

In the ruling party in Nigeria, Peoples Democratic Party(PDP),

Zainab Maina holds sway as part of the think-tank as Member, PDP Elders Committee; Member, PDP Board of Trustees; Executive Director, Women Affairs of the Jonathan/Sambo Presidential Campaign(2010);

Member, PDP Presidential Electoral/Screening Committee(2010); National Women Representative, PDP Presidential Campaign Council(2007); Delegate, National Political Reform Conference (NPRC)-2005; Women Representative, PDP Reconciliation Committee on theExecutive/Legislative Impasse(2002); International Convener, Home Economics and Consumer Affairs International Council of Women (ICW) Bangkok, Thailand(1993).

Her Non-Governmental Work Activities
- Founder/President, Women for Peace Initiative (WOPI)
- Nigeria Patron, Young Muslim Women Association, Nigeria Sub-Regional Coordinator- Anglophone Africa,
- International Council for Women Member
- World Association of NGOs (WANGO) Member, West African Civil Society Forum (WACSOF)
- INGO Ambassador, International Non-Governmental Organisation(London, UK)

Awards and Honours

National Award of Excellence towards Women Development

Abuja, Nigeria Jean Harris Award – Rotary International Winner of the Distinguished Eagle Achievement Award Newark, New Jersey, USA Amazon Women Award for Contribution towards the Development of Womanhood, Lagos, Nigeria. Africa Youth Congress Award on the authority of the Senate Headquarters, Banjul, the Gambia Merit Award by the Mayor of Atlanta, USA Meritorious Certificate for Loyal and Devoted Services to Development by the Nawar-U-Deen Society of Nigeria Certificate of Recognition – University of Kansas, Lawrence, USA Quintessence Award for Remarkable Contribution to Humanity by media in support of Humanity (MISH) Ambassador for peace by the Universal Peace Federation and the Inter-Religious and International federation for world peace Honorary citizen of Kansas City, USA Fellow, African Business School – FABS Fellow chartered Institute of Administration – FCIA Member of the Order of the Federal Republic – MFR.

OBIAGELI "OBY" EZEKWESILI

Obiageli "Oby" Ezekwesili, a Nigerian national, joined the World Bank, as Vice President of the Africa Region on May 1, 2007. Oby's unique blend of first-hand experiences, especially in the more challenging and complex areas of energy sector reform and education, position her well to deal with the many challenges in Africa. A critical factor in Oby's leadership style is her ability to achieve client "buy-in" no matter how extensive the reform strategy presented. Oby's life is a testament to her dedication to Africa as is the high degree of respect in which she is held by the international community. Her passion for and commitment to Africa, her high degree of integrity and her optimism brings strengths to the Region.

Background

Obiageli Ezekwesili, a Nigerian national, joined the World Bank from her position as Minister of Education within the Government of Nigeria. Oby has a rich resume with hands-on experience and accomplishments in a unique mix of private sector, civil society and public sector positions. Oby began her career as an auditor and management consultant, where she focused on financial planning, SME financing, audit and regulatory compliance. From 1994 to 1999, she served as one of the founding members of Transparency International where she held the position Director, Africa. In 2000, she went on to serve as Special Assistant to the President of Nigeria on Budget Monitoring, and the Price Intelligence Unit, where she spear-headed institutional reforms through the establishment of due process mechanisms and strategies. In this capacity, Oby achieved previously unheard of success by markedly reducing both procurement costs to the Government and turnaround time for completion of Government projects, while improving transparency.

Oby subsequently served as Minister of Solid Minerals Development, with emphasis on reforming Nigeria's mining sector to internationally recognised standards, especially in the area of policy transparency, with the purpose of increasing levels of global investment, and investor confidence, in the sector. She provided leadership in the drafting of the Nigerian Minerals and Mining Act, establishing the Nigerian Mining Cadastre Office and opening up Nigeria's mining sector to private participation. Oby has also served as the Chairperson for the Nigeria Extractive Industries Transparency Initiative since 2004 and pioneered the voluntary sign-on of Nigeria to the EITI Principles, as well as the first ever audit of the oil and gas sector.

While she was Minister of Education, she was tasked with leading the country's on-going comprehensive reform strategy within the education sector. She restructured and refocused the ministry for the attainment of EFA targets and MDGs, introduced Public Private Partnership models for service delivery, revamped the Federal Inspectorate Service as an improved quality assurance mechanism and introduced transparency and accountability mechanisms for better governance of the budget. The track record attesting to Oby's innovative success in this area culminated with the Nigerian stock exchange launch of "Adopt-A-Public School Initiative". Oby holds a Masters in International Law & Diplomacy from University of Lagos, along with a Masters of Public Administration from the Kennedy School of Government, Harvard. She is also a chartered accountant.

MARGARET EKPO (1914-2006)

Margaret Ekpo was born in Creek Town, Cross River State to the family of Okoroafor Obiasulor and Inyang Eyo Aniemewue. In 1946, she had the opportunity to study abroad at Rathmines School of Domestic Economics (now DIT Aungier Street), Dublin. She received a diploma in domestic science and on her return to Nigeria, she established a Domestic Science and Sewing institute in Aba.

Margaret Ekpo's first direct participation in political ideas and associations was in 1945. She organised a Market Women Association in Aba to unionise market women in the city. She used the association to promote women solidarity as a platform to fight for the economic rights of women, economic protections, and the expansionary political rights of women. Margaret Ekpo's awareness of growing movements for civil rights for women around the world prodded her into demanding the same for the women in her country and to fight the discriminatory and oppressive political and civil role colonialism played in the subjugation of women. She felt that women abroad were already fighting for civil rights and had more voice in political and civil matters than their counterparts in Nigeria. In the 1950's she also teamed up with Funmilayo Ransome Kuti to protest against killings at an Enugu coal mine. In 1953, she was nominated by the N.C.N.C to the regional House of Chiefs and in 1954, she established the Aba Township Women's Association. She won a seat into the Eastern Regional House of Assembly in 1961. A position that allowed her to fight for issues affecting women at the time. After a military coup ended the first republic, she took a less prominent approach to politics. In 2001, the Calabar Airport was named after her.

FUNMILAYO RANSOME KUTI (1900-1978)

Funmilayo Ransome Kuti was born on 25th October 1900 in Abeokuta, Nigeria. She attended the Abeokuta Grammar school and later went to England for further studies. She soon returned and became a teacher. Her political activism led to her being described as "The Mother of Africa". Early on, she was a very powerful force advocating for the Nigerian woman's right to vote. Throughout her career, she was known as an educator and activist. In 1949, she led a protest against Native Authorities, especially the Alake of Egbaland. In 1953, she founded the Federation of Nigerian Women Societies which subsequently formed an alliance with the Women's International Democratic Federation. She was one of the few women elected to the House of Chiefs. Among other things, Funmilayo Ransome Kuti organised workshops for illiterate market women. She also oversaw the successful abolishing of separate tax rates for women. She received the national honour of membership in the Order of Niger in 1965; The University of Ibadan also bestowed upon her the Honorary Doctorate of Laws in 1968. Funmilayo Kuti was the mother of the activists Late Fela Anikulapo Kuti, a musician,

Beko Ransome Kuti, a doctor, and Professor Olikoye Ransome Kuti, a doctor and a former health minister of Nigeria. In old age, her activism was over-shadowed by that of her three sons, who provided opposition to various Nigerian military juntas. In 1978, Funmilayo was thrown from a second floor window in her son Fela's compound when the place was stormed by one thousand armed military personnel. She lapsed into a coma in February of that year, and died on 13 April 1978, as a result of her injuries.

HAJIA GAMBO SAWABA (1933-2001)

Hajia Gambo Sawaba was born in 1933 to the family of Fatima and Isa Amarteifo. She was educated at the Native Authority Primary School in Tudun Wada. She was a Nigerian politician and activist who was a supporter of the Northern Elements Progressive Union during the first republic. She was one of the early members of NEPU in Zaria. Her political activities during that period earned her persecutions from both the colonial authorities and the native administrations which resulted in her being incarcerated for more than a dozen times. Her first political incident with the law occurred in Kano where she was sent to help NEPU with canvassing for women support. As soon as the reports of her activities reached the emir, she was arrested and tried by an Alkali court. She was convicted and sent to prison.

After her release, she went public with the appalling prison conditions but that also got her arrested again and she was later asked to leave Kano by the Emir.

She is also known for some of her charitable causes and also for her views on women liberation in the arena of politics. Through the first republic, she continued with her political activities sometimes suffering humiliating punishments from opposition thugs. She supported a woman's right to vote and was elected leader of the women's wing of NEPU.

Chapter Nine

THE WHOLE WOMAN

"The most common way people give up their power is by thinking they don't have any."

Alice Walker

Women empowerment does not only involve, entrepreneurship, financial freedom or even gender equality. Instead, it is a healthy combination of all these things that makes a woman complete. It has a lot to do with self-esteem, self-image and self-perception as well. Women are sensitive beings and are made in a delicate, yet strong way. A woman is empowered when she is assertive, has value for herself and believes in herself.

Barbara Klein, professor of women's studies at Oberlin College and director of a study which revealed that women are now empowered by virtually everything the typical woman does, says, "From what she eats for breakfast to the way she cleans her home, today's woman lives in a state of near-constant empowerment". As recently as 15 years ago, a woman could only feel empowered by advancing in a male-dominated work world, asserting her own wants and needs against all odds, or even pushing for a stronger voice in politics. There's a whole lot of difference today as a woman can empower herself through actions as seemingly inconsequential as driving her children to the games or watching TV.

This book focuses on the economic empowerment of women but does not overlook the fact that beauty and expression are parts of female empowerment. Here are some ideas to empower yourself as a woman, economically, emotionally, physically and in all ramifications.

Learn

Never stop learning. Freeing and expanding your mind is the first step toward empowering yourself, so educate yourself in any way you can. Even if you don't have a formal education there are still plenty of ways to increase your knowledge on your own. Taking the initiative to teach yourself something new is one of the most empowering things you can do. Read books, go to the library or a bookstore, join a book club, or do research on the Internet. And if you are a busy mom with no time to take a class, check out an educational book from the library and read a few pages before bed each night. A smart woman is an empowered woman.

Be Independent

Being comfortable with who you are, and knowing that you are strong enough to face any situation on your own, is an empowering feeling. Do not let things like your marital or economic status stop you from doing everything you want to do. Make it a goal to try something new that you wouldn't normally do alone. While you're out there 'living it up' you'll be building confidence and increasing your chances at achieving your dreams.

Dream Big

Don't be afraid to go after your dreams. No dream is too big or unobtainable. An empowered woman knows that she can accomplish anything she sets out to do, it is simply a matter of perseverance, believing in yourself and following your heart. If you truly believe in your dreams you can make them happen. But in order to do this you must try. Consider making a vision board to illustrate and remind yourself of all the goals you would like to accomplish.

Value yourself and relationships where you are an equal

In any relationship, there is going to be give-and-take as situations and circumstances change, but you should also feel that, overall, your value in the partnership is equal to that of your partner's. Never feel or allow yourself to be treated any less than you deserve.

Speak up about sexist jokes or sexist images

Promote sexual harassment policies in your workplace or in your environment. Do not let snide remarks about women or derogatory statements about women go unchallenged.

Focus on the person instead appearance

To foster a healthier self-image, compliment yourself or other women for achievements, thoughts and actions and not necessarily the quality of their appearance.

Expose and understand unrealistic media images for what they are: retouched, computer-manipulated photos of models - a group that makes up only a tiny subset of the population.

Learn how to ask and negotiate for wages and raises

If you are a working class woman, know the worth of your job. Education is your best defence Research everything you can think of to find the competitive salary for your job in your region - employment surveys, libraries, professional organisations, peers etc. For a raise, you need evidence to show your boss that you deserve it. One way to document your contribution to your company is to keep a job diary. Every week, or even every day, write down what you did and how it helped meet the company's objectives. Remember that attributes such as positive attitude, willingness to put in overtime and quality of work are essential.

Think about, plan and prepare for career advancement

Mentors are a great asset. If your company doesn't offer clear career ladders, research or find a seminar to help you understand your industry and opportunities.

Encourage risk taking

People develop self-reliance when they're given the space to solve problems and make mistakes in the process.

It is great to be a female athlete, senator or physician as the case may be. But we must not overlook the homemaker who spends most of the day at home tending to the needs of her family, or the single mom who works two jobs to maintain a good standard of living for her children or even the female college student who takes on odd jobs to pay her way through school. Only by lauding every single thing a woman does, no matter how ordinary, can they truly experience empowerment.

Conclusion

"Entrepreneurship...is about turning what excites you in life into capital, so that you can do more of it and move forward with it"

Richard Branson

Women, by nature, have creative abilities, are blessed with the ability to persist and pursue their desires and are patient nurturers of children. This tenacity is usually transferred into business where women are great innovators, have the ability to develop passion for what they believe in and hang in there for the long haul. All in all, women are able to start small and hang in there until they build great enterprises. Take Martha Stewart, Oprah Winfrey, Mary Kay Ash or even the 'Mammy Benzs' of West Africa; each entrepreneurial woman takes her passion and turns it into a global, viable, and vibrant enterprise!

The economic empowerment of women is very crucial for poverty reduction. When women are financially empowered, then, the tendency to create ideas and initiatives on how to support their families, develop their communities, states and nation increase. Generally, Nigerian women have not really enjoyed equal economic participation with their male counterparts, however the empowerment of women as entrepreneurs within business and the working world is something that has slowly, but steadily developed over the years. The Administration of former President Olusegun Obasanjo made significant steps to empower women within business and the work place. Under the former President, the Federal Government made several efforts and introduced various measures to reflect a good percentage of women in governance starting with the appointment of six female cabinet ministers as soon as he assumed office in 1999. Arguably his Administration, was one of the most gender sensitive in history, President Obasanjo stated:

"Gender Equality is one of the fundamental principles of the Commonwealth, and I would like to emphasize that gender equality is achievable and with your numerical strength, women can and indeed are making a difference in governance in Nigeria. Given such numerical strength, Nigeria cannot afford to allow such abundant, qualified and skilled resources of women to be wasted. This Administration fully supports the efforts to balance gender representation and recommits itself to exercise the necessary political will to ensure that more women are appointed at all decision-making levels."

Under his leadership, several female civil servants reached the peak of their careers as became Ambassadors or Heads of Foreign Missions some became Director-Generals and Permanent Secretaries.

More recently the current President Goodluck Jonathan launched a Public Works and Women/Youth Employment (PW/WYE) project.The project aims to generate around 370,000 jobs across the country over the next few months. The President said:

"...the SURE Programme seeks to target the largest population of unskilled unemployed and under employed poor women and youths as well as other vulnerable groups in our society by presenting them with ample opportunities in the public works programmes and internships in firms for the skilled and educated. The project is designed to create immediate employment opportunities for women and youths in labour intensive public works."

In February 2012 the Central Bank of Nigeria (CBN) disclosed that it planned to introduce a women economic empowerment scheme that would make sure that female entrepreneurs could access credit from banks at single-digit rates of interest by the end of the year; and roll out a three-year programme that would seek to empower women bankers in the financial system as well. CBN stated that the Bankers Committee had set a target between 2012 and 2014 to ensure that 40 percent of top management positions in banks and 30 percent of board positions in all banks are held by women.

As stated at the beginning of this book, women's empowerment not only provides women with the power to act on their own behalf, it also ensures that those actions have a positive impact on their homes, communities, nations and the globe. As women become entrenched in the political-economic fabric of their countries, they make tremendous impact that facilitates such turnarounds as the Rwandan story. With each female entrepreneur jobs are created, families are cared for, infrastructures are built, resources are generated, and communities are grown. What is more, every woman spreads her entrepreneurial fervour to others until entire communities are lifted out of poverty as we see evolving in Bangladesh, India, and Rwanda. And the governments of these states are with them every step of the way. For example, the government of Rwanda continues to lead initiatives that promote the status of women in the country and improve the way of doing business in general.

References (APA Format)

Gender Pay Gap. (2011, July 22). In Wikipedia, the free Encyclopedia. Retrieved July 23, 2011, fromhttp://en.wikipedia.org/wiki/Gender_pay_gap Equal Pay for Women. (2011, July 5).

In Wikipedia, the free Encyclopedia. Retrieved July 23, 2011, fromhttp://en.wikipedia.org/wiki/Equal_pay_act Equal Pay act of 1963. (2011, June 16). In Wikipedia, the free Encyclopedia.

Retrieved July 23, 2011, fromhttp://en.wikipedia.org/wiki/Equal_pay_act Kelly Rathje. (2008). Male Versus Female Earnings – Is the Gender Wage Gap Converging?: . The Expert Witness. Retrieved from http://www.economica.ca/ew07_1p2.htm

Pay Equity Legislation in Canada. (2011) Human resources and skills development. Retrieved from http://www.hrsdc.gc.ca/eng/labour/labour_law/esl/pay_equity.shtml

Measuring the impact of Women's economic Development. (2011). International centre for research and development.

Retrieved from http://www.icrw.org/where-we-work/measuring-impact-women%E2%80%99s-economic-development-programs

Women's economic Empowerment. (Dec 2010). Trends and good practices on women's entrepreneurship in the OSCE region. Retrieved from http://www.osce.org/gender/75553

Appendix 1

Entrepreneurship Quiz

Instructions: Read each question and pick the answer that most accurately describes your behaviour, feeling or attitude as it actually is, not as you would like it to be or think it should be. You must be honest with yourself to get a valid score.

Are you a Self-Starter?
1. Easy does it. I don't put myself out until I have to.
2. If someone gets me started, I keep going all right.
3. I do things my own way. Nobody needs to tell me when to get going.

How do you feel about other people?
1. Most people annoy me.
2. I have enough friends and I don't need anybody else.
3. I like people. I can get along with just about anybody.

Can you lead others?
1. I usually let someone else get things moving.
2. I can get people to do things if I drive them.
3. I can get most people to go along with me without much difficulty.

Can you take responsibility?
1. There's always some show off around waiting to take over. I let him.
2. I'll take over if I have to, but I'd rather let someone else be responsible.
3. I take charge of and see things through.

How good an organiser are you?
1. I just take things as they come.
2. I do all right unless things get too complicated. Then I get out of it.
3. I like to have a plan before I start. I'm usually the one who lines things up.

How good a worker are you?
1. I can't see that hard work gets you anywhere.
2. I'll work hard for a time, but when I'm tired, that's it.
3. I can keep going as long as necessary. I don't mind working hard.

Can you make decisions?
1. I don't like to be the one who decides things. I'd probably blow it.
2. I can if I have plenty of time. If I have to make up my mind fast, I usually regret it.
3. I can make up my mind in a hurry if necessary, and my decision is usually O.K.

Can people trust what you say?

1. What's the big deal if the other person doesn't know the difference?
2. I try to speak the truth, but sometimes I just say what is easiest.
3. People can trust what I say. I don't say things I don't mean.

Can you stick with whatever you start?

1. If a job doesn't go right, I turn off. Why beat your brains out?
2. If I make up my mind to do something, I don't let anything stop me.
3. I usually finish what I start.

Can you keep records?

1. Records are not important. I know what needs to be known without keeping records.
2. I can, but it's more important to get the work done than to shuffle numbers.
3. Since they are needed I'll keep records even though I don't want to.

Scoring: If you picked mostly A, you need to improve your attitude in order to develop an entrepreneurial mindset. In order to be successful in business, you must learn to take initiative, work hard, and keep good records. Take heart, the skills you need can be learnt.

If you picked mostly B, you have qualities of a successful entrepreneur with some weak spots. As you read this book, discover your weak spots and create a plan to overcome them – either get required training or hire someone else to do the work.

If you picked mostly C, you definitely have what it takes to succeed in a small business of your own, don't waste time thinking too hard, your way to business success is wide open!

Appendix 2

Business Plan Template

(Your business plan should include the following sections especially if you intend to obtain a loan. Fill in the blank spaces).

Executive Summary (write this after you have written all the other sections. It is simply a summary of your business concept):

Business Description (what is your company established to do?)

Products and Services (what would you be offering the public and in what format?)

Marketing Plan (how do you plan to sell your products? Refer to Appendices 1 and 2):

Management and Personnel (how would you run your business?):

Financial Investment Data (What funds would you need to start and where do you plan to get your funding? How would you continue to invest capital into your business?):

Financial Plan (Paint a larger picture of your day-to-day expenses beyond your initial start up costs):

Appendices (attach other important documents):

Appendix 3

250 HOME BUSINESS IDEAS FOR WOMEN

ART HOME BUSINESS

1. Airbrush Artist
2. Art Dealer
3. Desktop Publishing
4. Engraving
5. EBook Cover Artist
6. Fashion Designer
7. Freelance Artist
8. Graphic Artist
9. Monogrammer
10. Photographer
11. Sign Painting Business

BUSINESS

12. Accountant
13. Advertising Consultant
14. Answering Service
15. Attorney
16. Billing Service
17. Bookkeeping
18. Brand Consultant

19. Business/Marketing Plan Developer
20. Business Plan Consultant
21. Business Referral Consultant
22. Business Analyst
23. Business Coach
24. Business Writer
25. Financial Advisor
26. Information Broker
27. Internet Marketing Professional
28. Inventory Service
29. Job Search Service Provider
30. Medical Transcriber
31. Medical Billing
32. Newsletter Writer/Designer
33. Process Server'
34. Professional Practice Consultant
35. Project Development Manager
36. Promotion Service Provider
37. Office Support Administrator
38. Tax Preparer/Advisor
39. Temporary Help Services
40. Virtual Assistant

DAY CARE AND CARE-GIVING WORK AT HOME BUSINESS

41.   Day Care for Children
42.   Day Care for Seniors
43.   Day Care for Adults
44.   Dating Services
45.   Home Health Care
46.   Home Based Hair/Nail Salon
47.   Masseuse
48.   Personal Fitness Trainer
49.   Personal Weight Management Consultant
50.   Reflexologist

CLEANING

51.   Homeowners Referral
52.   House Cleaning Service
53.   Professional Organizing Service
54.   Garage Cleaning
55.   Carpet Cleaning
56.   Janitorial Services

BUSINESS COACHES AND PERSONAL COACHES:

57.   Business Coach
58.   Career Counselor

59. Exercise Consultant

60. Motivational Speaker

61. Marketing Coach

62. PC Coaching (Personal Computer)

63. Personal Coach

64. Technology Coach

65. Stress Management Coach

66. Time Management Consultant

67. Weight loss Coach

COOKING:

68. Caterer for Weddings, Parties, etc

69. Canning Service

70. Cake Decorator

71. Cooking School

72. Cookie Basket Gift Service

73. Create and Market your own Special Recipe

74. Elderly Meals Preparer

75. Food Delivery Service

76. Personal Chef

77. Write your own Cookbook

78. Chef Agency

COMPUTERS

79. Affiliate Manager
80. Browser Sizing Consultant
81. Candy Bar Wrapper Designer
82. Computer Technician
83. Computer Programmer
84. Desktop Publisher
85. EBook Software Developer
86. EBook Compiler
87. EBook Publisher
88. Ecommerce Marketing Directory
89. HTML Newsletter Designer
90. Internet Researcher
91. Internet Portal Services
92. Link Checking Services
93. Link Generating Services
94. Multimedia Specialist
95. Online Instructor
96. Online Store Owner
97. Online Tech Support
98. Newsletter Promotion
99. Search Engine Positioning Specialist
100. Software Developer
101. Systems Integrator
102. Teleclass Leader
103. Website Designer

104. Website Programmer
105. Virtual Assistant
106.

CRAFTS

107. Airbrush Art
108. Calligraphy
109. Candle Making
110. Chair Caning, Rushwork and Weaving
111. Craft Kits
112. Basket Weaving
113. Dollhouses
114. Framing
115. Furniture Painter/Artist
116. Greeting Cards
117. Jewelry
118. Photography
119. Pot Pouri & Scented Crafts
120. Scrapbooking Service
121. Silk Flower Arranging
122. Woodworker
123. Wreath Creations

DELIVERY

124. After-School Child Pickup
125. Errand Service
126. Elderly Driving Service
127. Groceries Delivery Services
128. Mail/Package Delivery
129. Meal Delivery Service
130. Moving Service
131. Personal Shopper
132. Prescription Pickup/Delivery
133. Take-out Delivery
134. Taxi Service
135. Light/Heavy Goods Courier Service

ENTERTAINMENT

136. Cake Decorator
137. Candy Bar Wrapper Designer
138. Clown Services
139. Children's Party Planner
140. Food Caterer
141. Game Inventor
142. School Program and Assemblies
143. Tour Services
144. Novelty Message Service
145. Wedding Planner

146. Reunion Coordinator (Class/Family)
147. Garage Sale Coordinator
148. Business Seminar Coordinator
149. Party Decorator
150. Party Rentals
151. Singing Telegram Service
152. Trade Show Planner
153. Yard Signs Service (New Baby, Birthdays, Retirement, etc.

GARDENING

154. Home Owners Referral
155. Gardening Services
156. Landscaping Services
157. Environmental Services
158. Gardening Consultant
159. Growing Herbs
160. Florist
161. Fresh Flower
162. Farmers Market -selling produce
163. Organic Gardener
164. Wreath Designer

HEALTHCARE

165. Elderly Care Services
166. Home Health Care
167. Medical Billing
168. Medical Transcriptionist
169. Organic Gardener
170. Personal Fitness Trainer
171. Personal Weight Management Consultant
172. Post-Natal Care Help
173. Nutritionist
174. Sales in Health/Nutritional/Allergy Products
175. Reflexologist
176. Work-at-Home Nurses

HOME SERVICES

177. Blind Cleaning
178. Carpets and Rug Cleaning
179. Realtor
180. Garage Sales Coordinator
181. Gardening/Landscaping
182. Home Owners Referral
183. House sitting
184. Housekeeper
185. Interior Design
186. Office Cleaner

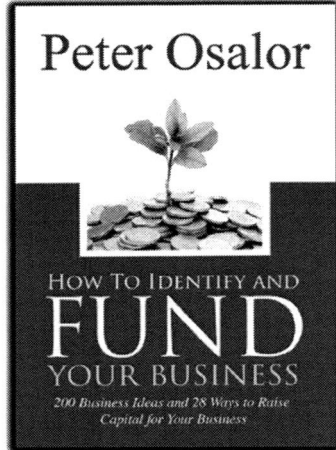

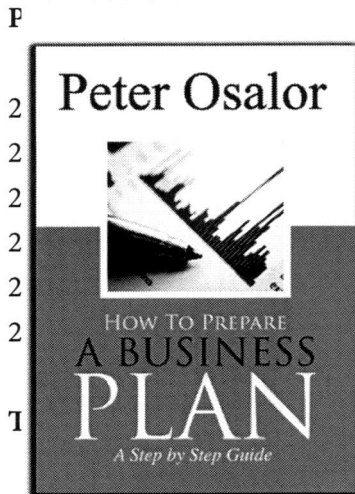

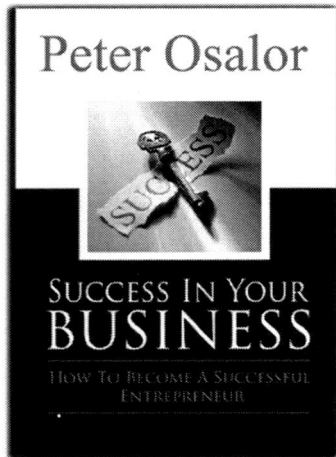

P

2
2
2
2
2
2
2

P

2
2
2
2
2
2

T

The
Entrepreneurial
Revolution
A solution for poverty eradication

Peter Osalor FCCA, CTA

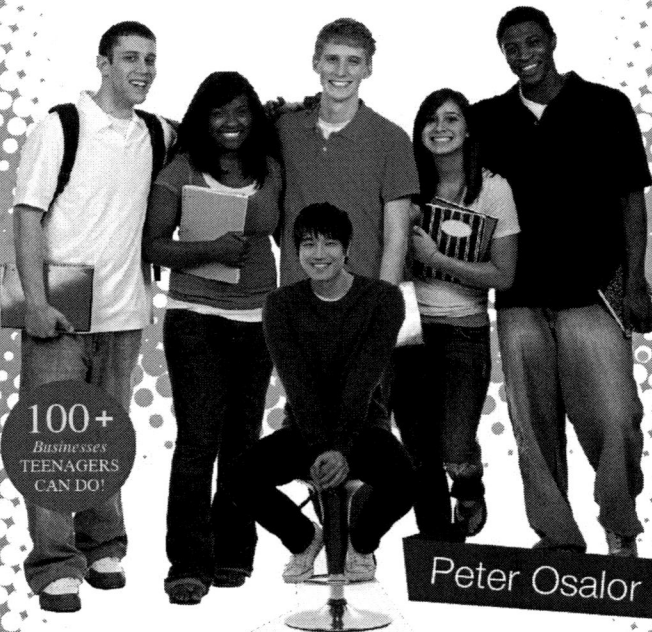

50⁺

YEAR OLD
ENTREPRENEURS

Fulfilling Your Dreams In Your Golden Years.
It's Never Too Late!

200
Businesses
YOU
CAN DO!

Peter Osalor

50 PROVEN CURES FOR POVERTY

CURES FOR

POVERTY

ENTREPRENEURS, ENTREPREPRENEURIALISM AND THE FREE MARKET

"Time *tested* principles for transforming your *environment*"

Peter Osalor

Peter Osalor

ECONOMIC
TRANSFORMATION

From a Poor Person to a Wealthy Person,
From a Poor Nation to a Wealthy Nation

Entrepreneur, Entrepreneurship, Entrepreneulism,
MSME, Entrepreneurial Revolution

COMING SOON